A Biblical Introduction to
THE OLD TESTAMENT

Contemporary Catechetics
Series

In this brief but comprehensive study of the Old Testament, Professor Gross offers the catechist and others the opportunity to benefit from the most recent biblical research.

The modern catechist need no longer be simply an instructor by rote if he employs the knowledge offered by biblical scholars. As the development of kerygmatic hermeneutics becomes established, the disunity between catechetical instruction and theological knowledge will recede.

Through a more vivid, and accurate, understanding of the place and background of the Old Testament books the modern reader can better appreciate the significance and function of these writings. Herein is not found a complete study of the methods of exegesis or of the methods of catechetics. Rather this book is addressed to the catechist to convince him of the importance of biblical testimonies and to enable him to cope with the dependence of the message upon human and historical conditions.

The termination of our study of the Old Testament is found in Old Testament theology—the transition of the world of faith of the Old Testament into a system which presents the Bible itself and which so places its accents that the graduated importance of the teachings is underlined as the Bible itself requests it."

Thus, Professor Gross provides his reader with an orientation that will lead him to appreciate the vital connection between the Old and the New Testaments as found in the supernatural salvation plan of God.

JOSEF GOLDBRUNNER
Series Editor

A Biblical Introduction To
The Old Testament [36]

HEINRICH GROSS

UNIVERSITY OF NOTRE DAME PRESS
Notre Dame

NIHIL OBSTAT:
Joseph Hoffman, C.S.C.,
Censor Deputatus

IMPRIMATUR:
✠Leo A. Pursley, D.D.,
Bishop of Fort Wayne-South Bend
March 15, 1968

Original German Title:

KLEINE BIBELKUNDE ZUM ALTEN TESTAMENT
First published by Kösel-Verlag, Munich, 1967

CONTENTS

GENERAL CONSIDERATIONS

I

THE OLD TESTAMENT AS PART OF THE BIBLE

No other book of world literature enjoys such widespread fame as the Bible. In its Old and New Testament form it has been the foundation for all Christian denominations. Moreover, the Old Testament, the sacred book of the Jewish religion, has contributed greatly to the development of the Koran upon which Mohammendanism is based.

The word "bible" derives from the Phoenician city of Gebal (Ezk 27:9), situated forty kilometers north of Beirut, which the Greeks called "Byblos"—then the most important port for shipping Egyptian papyrus, from whence its name. The Greek word *byblos* signified the collective noun not only for writing materials but also for scrolls and codices. Finally it became the preferred designation for biblical writings and has penetrated the Western languages via the Latin. In Greek *byblos* simply means "book."

Later the Bible became known as "Scripture" or "Holy Writ" (2 Tm 3:15), which shows that this is not a single book but rather a collection of books that are distinguished by the adjective "holy."

The Latin word *testament*—which actually means a last will—is the translation of a Hebrew expression that generally is rendered by our word "covenant" or "alliance." With that term we touch the very core of these books, for in their center is God's convenant with his people.

That characteristic of the Bible which is expressed in its very name lies at the heart of it where God acts and speaks. By revealing his salvific work for mankind God also reveals himself, and this revelation comes down to us in a twofold manner: in tradition and in Holy Scripture.

Thus the Bible not only contains the general truths about God, world, and man as a result of divine revelation, but also proclaims the message of *salvation* which God has undertaken for this world in space and time,

4

that is, in history. It shows how God's plan of salvation was realized through the slow growth of a people *chosen by him*. The purpose of this plan is to unite all men with God and make them *full citizens of his kingdom*. This is the goal that is pursued by all the books of the Bible and is apparent in revelation itself. Yet this purpose is not being sought in a sudden and fast-moving ascent, but by a gradual progress through time during which men should be led toward the kingdom prepared for them by God. In the center of this promised gift of salvation, of course, stands Christ.

The Scriptures of the Old Testament proclaim how God has furthered the history of the chosen people of Israel—through a tortuous path—intervening and judging often. From many angles this history points to the Messiah who is to appear in the fullness of time. This dimension of the future runs through the Old Testament like a bright red thread: it is fashioned in manifold and various promises and seems to stamp the Old Testament with its peculiar trait—that of lumping the history of Israel under the sign of a leading idea and making of it a history of salvation, namely, a history caused and governed by God in the course of which he makes his people participate in salvation. In short, the main thrust is aimed toward communicating his message of salvation to the people whose history he is fashioning.

The New Testament tells of the fulfillment, here and now, of this "Good News" of God's ordering of "eternal redemption" through Jesus Christ in the heart of time. This redemption is achieved for the peoples of all times. Here salvation history not only evolves in time but also progresses from stage to stage until it reaches its fullest development.[1] In the midst of this history is the kingdom of God, hidden but growing quietly until it comes forth at the end of time in all its glory, and the course of this salvation history enters the perpetual now of eternity, the "place of rest" (Ps 95).

II

OUTLINE OF THE OLD TESTAMENT CANON

The entire Bible consists of seventy-two books; of these, forty-five form the Old Testament. According to the main contents of these books we divide them into groups of twenty-one historical, seven didactic, and seventeen prophetic. This number, expressly fixed by the Council of Trent, is based on the so-called Septuagint Canon and enumerates an additional seven scriptures beyond the Palestinian Canon which are known as the deutero-canonical books. Protestant demoninations generally follow the orientation of the Palestinian Canon.

Not only is it the number of biblical books that distinguishes the Septuagint from the concept of the Hebrew Bible, but also its order and its subdivision of groups are different. The Hebrew Bible distinguishes the Torah (Law)—Pentateuch, the five-volume book; the Prophets—earlier prophets, historical books outside the Pentateuch; later prophets, the scriptural prophets; and the writings or pedagogic books. The authentic list of biblical books as set down by the Council of Trent is called the "Canon of Holy Scriptures." The word *canon* in this context implies authenticity; it means that it is an official catalogue of biblical writings.

Hence, the authentic interpretation of the above-mentioned scriptures is referred to the magisterium of the Church, whose task it is to insert into the official canon only those books that are inspired. Thus the magisterium, by fixing and delimiting the biblical canon, has full control over the books in question.

During the first three centuries after Christ the general magisterium of the Church carried out this work. However, it was not until the Synod of Hippo in 393 that the idea of the canon had first been questioned. And this question had assumed much greater importance during the Reformation when inconsistencies within the canon were being proved. During its fourth session, April 8, 1546, the Council of Trent had reaffirmed solemnly the extent of the biblical canon as fixed for centuries and listed every single one of the seventy-two books as canonical.

It would then be wrong to assume that the Old Testament has canonical rank and validity only because the synagogue considered it as Holy Writ. As canonical scriptures, the Old Testament has for us the same rank as the New Testament because Christ and his apostles held it as such. The Church faithfully followed this concept. Moreover, it was not until about 90 A.D. that a Jewish authority, under Rabbi Akiba, had definitely determined for the synagogue the borders of the Old Testament Canon, which until then had remained undefined.

III

REDACTION OF THE OLD
TESTAMENT

In order to take up this question and answer it, we must bear in mind that the Old Testament is a collection of forty-five individual writings and that the Bible greatly differs in its development from any modern book. At the beginning of biblical tradition we find the word of God and his work imposed upon man by way of the prophets, who were chosen by God himself to act as guides for the life of his people. As it came to be more and more recognized that not only the actual present but the future as well was being fashioned by the word of God, all these vital traditions began to be written down and eventually were formed into whole biblical books. The Old Testament serves as a source of literary expression for the life of God's chosen people according to history and as it actually was according to God's will to be lived out. Thus we can easily comprehend how the Old Testament book has grown over a thousand years. The oldest main texts certainly can be traced to the founder of the Old Testament religion, Moses, to about 1200 B.C. The preface to Sirach, the last book of the Old Testament, can be dated about the year 132 B.C.

This long span of development finds justification not in the absence of literary genius among the Israelites, but in the long and fruitful history which God has conducted with his chosen people. God's plan of salvation materializes gradually, step-by-step, into visible forms. With this in mind, we will indeed find it quite understandable that the Bible cannot couch its proclamations and narratives in the form of a catechism. The Bible—unlike a catechism which presents the deposit of faith and ethics in a well-ordered, factual system—connot do without the perspective of time, for it must trace the history of revelation as it developed. A peculiar characteristic of revelation is that it takes place in a historical frame. Throughout his plan of salvation God from time to time intervenes into the course of history: he calls at providential times men of his choice and commands them to bring to the people a specific mandate so as to continue the revelation process. It is through these designated ones that he gives new points of departure and new beginnings, that he determines a new direction to be followed by his people. In such critical moments of this unique course of history God has called prophets, judges, kings, and priests who have deposited the inspired words given them into books that were later named after them.

It remains the ineffable secret of God why such a long and often confusing development of Israel's history was necessary to transmit the deposit of revelation of the Old Testament. In spite of it, it is surprising how the language of the Old Testament has remained vigorous and plastic over thousands of years— so much so that it was able to receive and express the many different and various individual revelations—and how the continuity and progress of salvation history has been preserved. Thus has the Old Testament grown with, and from, the life of the chosen people with its God; on the other hand it also presents the guidelines and attitudes for Israel's life according to God and takes care that the direction which the development is taking follows carefully God's plan.

IV

LANGUAGE AND TEXT OF
THE OLD TESTAMENT

Most of the books of the Old Testament have been written in the Hebrew language, with some parts in the related Aramaic (the language of Jesus), largely in the books of Esdras and Daniel. By the way, the seven co-called deutero-canonical books and the additions to Esther and Daniel have come down to us only in Greek; these include Tobit, Judith, Baruch, Wisdom, Sirach, and the two books of Maccabees. Protestants usually fall back on the Palestinian Canon and refer to the seven deutero-canonical books as apocryphal works. (We call those books "apocryphal" that had their start about the same time as the biblical ones and treat biblical themes

15

without being Holy Writ. Protestant denominations usually refer to these works as pseudo-epigraphic.)

The original texts of Holy Scripture have all been lost. Even though the best texts of the critical editions of the Hebrew Bible are far from exact, they are on the whole reliable and in substance comparatively close to the original sources. There are not as many or as divergent variants as in the text traditions of the New Testament. We owe this mostly to the scholarly Masoretes, who from the fourth to the tenth centuries had done excellent work on the texts by producing the best forms on the basis of the oldest available manuscripts. Textual criticism has advanced greatly in modern times through the intensive explorations of the Dead Sea which are being researched for new biblical editions in their original form.

The best textual authority for the Old Testament is contained in the manuscripts of the Ben Ashi family, which during five or six generations, from 750 to 950, had done the main part of the Masorete work in Tiberias. The most important codex is that of Aleppo, which for some years has been the property of the University of Jerusalem and is now being issued for the first time as the basis for a critical text of the Old Testament undertaken by this university. Other significant codices are: *Codex Cairensis* at Cairo which comprises the earlier and later prophets; *Codex Leningradensis* at Leningrad, a complete Bible manuscript which was done in 1008; and the *Petersburg Prophets' Codex* from 916 which contains all scriptural prophets except Daniel.

After this short survey of the Old Testament's characteristics we shall now analyze the individual books or groups of books along with the question which modern research is most interested in and which may form the nucleus of further biblical-theological revelation.

SPECIAL INTRODUCTION

I

HISTORICAL BOOKS

1. THE PENTATEUCH—THE FIVE
BOOKS OF MOSES

Within Catholic circles, too, it is being recognized that the five books of Moses are not a literary work fused in one mold and that the theory of Wellhausen at the end of the nineteenth century which considered the Pentateuch as having originated from four sources should not be held completely erroneous. Protestant research has gone beyond Wellhausen, and these newly developed methods of form-, tradition-, and redaction-criticism make it possible for us to assume that these Pentateuchal sources—Yahwistic (J), Elohist (E), Deuteronomic (D), and the

Priestly (P)—may well have received their last redaction at the time Wellhausen believed they originated. All four strata—an expression which fits better than "sources"—must be viewed according to the depth dimension of their historical beginnings. The editors of the final composition have certainly injected theological concepts into all this immense material and thus given expression to their concrete understanding of God's salvific work.[1] In this, too, research has surpassed Wellhausen or, better, has deviated from his findings since it no longer understands the development of the Pentateuch with the help of Western philosophies, that is, with Hegel's philosophy of religion. By eliminating such blocks in the way of understanding, the Pentateuch issue has been cleared considerably in its religious and ideological aspects and can now be analyzed calmly and factually.

This in part sketches the task of present-day research: it means to determine the single sources not only with the tools of literary criticism, but to retrace the formation of the different epochs to investigate the specific statement of each in the light of its final form, and to integrate them into an overall understanding of the individual books or of the entire texts.

Analogously the deuteronomic works and chronicles are fitted into the books of Genesis, Exodus, Leviticus, and Numbers as historical works similar to the Pentateuch whose characteristics however are not quite clear and whose aims are not yet completely defined, as is the case with the other two historical works.

2. GENESIS

The fifty chapters of the first book are divided into two parts of greatly differing content. Though connected literally one to another, the first part (Gn 1–11), usually called primordial history, differs considerably from the second part, called the patriarchal narratives (Gn 12–50) both in theme and content.

Even though we generally have to consider the historiography of the Bible as a "tendentious" or "pragmatic" presentation of history distinguished from our critical historical method, the narratives in Genesis 1–11 occupy a special position if we consider the way biblical history was then written. They do not conform to any kind of historiography known to us but rather treat in a very condensed manner the primordial epochs for which there are no witnesses, or at least no profane ones. These chapters are based on sacred traditions which might even have originated with Abraham (probably 1750 B.C.) but which should be termed rather a prophetic retrospect than a reaching back to the beginnings of the ancient past.[2]

The first three chapters are of capital importance. Discussion is still going on as to whether next to the Priestly-scriptural report of creation (Gn 1,P), which by the use of a special verb *bārā'* traces everything created back to God without analogy, there might have been a second report on Yahweh's creation (Gn 2) or if Genesis 2 together with Genesis 3 rather belong to J which is intent on recording the initial situation of man, original sin, and the human condition in modern life that results from it. In any case man is shown as a creature of the All. Since the beginning of man's existence history exists, and his decision against God as a historical deed triggers important consequences for the future of all mankind.

From the traditions contained in the following chapters we may also conclude that human guilt and divine punishment formed the original history of mankind, that the magnificent possibilities offered in the beginning never became a reality, and that man and world continue to exist only because of God's patience and indulgence (Gn 8:21).

The lines of the narratives finally converge upon Abraham, with whom God inaugurates a new phase by opening a new way of salvation; here we have reached the atmosphere of a history—a patriarchal history—which can be traced at least in outline (Gn 12:50).

Theologically speaking, there is nowhere a greater rift than between Genesis 11 and 12, between primordial history and that of the patriarchs. The new approach God suggests to Abraham has for its aim *God's kingdom in a chosen people*. In order to make the new way quite clear, we witness at the beginning a command to the patriarch to dissolve all familiar and ethnic ties and to move to a strange country. At the same time, wandering and pilgrimage are revealed by God as existential. With this request God combines his promise of the great blessings which will be realized in numerous descendents: Abraham himself is destined to be the source and bearer of this blessing. This promise is realized in

God's convenant with Abraham—the single fact of choosing leads into the state of being chosen. It establishes God and the patriarch in a special relationship which assures him of God's constant benevolence and protection. This singular challenge is answered by Abraham with active faith when he delivers himself personally to God in every new situation. The highlight in the whole tradition of Abraham is reflected in the fact that, as the one chosen par excellence, he is according to Genesis 12–25 a model of the man completely united to God in faith (cf. Rm 4:16). Isaac's figure is not as well profiled (Gn 25–27) and signifies a transition to Jacob and his family. The texts show how the promise God made in the beginning is taking shape and how the physical as well as religious well-being of the sons of Abraham is safeguarded. Here the long narratives about Joseph prefigure the wisdom writings by pointing out in living example how the ideal image of man can be realized according to the religion of revelation.

Another question arises here. Up to our own times the historical indications of Genesis 12–50 aroused minimum belief, and the texts of the patriarchs were considered little more than old legends or folktale collections beyond which there was no historical truth for us to be reached. In the meantime—mostly thanks to archeology—a considerable change has been taking place. Today more and more the patriarchs are being contemplated as historical figures. The biblical tales of course do not inform us according to the possibilities and requirements of modern historiography, but the new findings present so much contemporary color that the prophets certainly cannot escape being regarded as the historical bearers of God's plan of salvation.[3]

3. EXODUS

In comparing Abraham's history with that of Israel—"when Israel was a child" (Ho 2:1) —there are astonishing similarities. Just as Abraham is called by God to go abroad and then led to Palestine and there brought specially close to him in the Covenant, so the salvation history of the people of Israel runs a parallel course though on a new and higher level. The identity in basic structure is of great importance for Bible theology and not at all accidental. In it is revealed the timeless law of the work of salvation and the kingdom of God to which the faithful of the New as well as the Old Testaments are subject; in it we recognize revelation's progressive course in spite of the many interruptions effected by man, a situation which God alone knows how to include in his salvation plan with all its human errors and discrepancies—according to the word of Joseph in Genesis 5:20, "You intended evil against me but God intended it for good."

Exodus describes in two main parts how Israel became the *people of God*. The first part (Ex 1–15) treats the captivity of Israel in the "Egyptian house of slavery," the call of Moses, his gigantic battle with Pharaoh and with it God's battle against the powers of the contemporary world, and the great work of redemption in the liberation from Egypt. These reports reflect the same Yahwistic, Elohist, and Priestly traditions, but now modern scholarship seems to take more serious note of the historical substratum and thus explicates the salvific significance of the event in constant relation to the historical happenings. As a matter of fact, chapter 12 in outlining the Passover is a classic example for the flowing together of historical events, salvation history significance, and cultic preparations. The deliverance from Egypt marked the later Old Testament literature as the basic salvific action, God's redemptive deed, a model of God's salvific action in general.

The liberation of Israel from Egypt leads to the Covenant on Mount Sinai in which God establishes the Old Testament religion (Ex 19–24). Essentially it consists of choosing the elect, pronouncing a covenant in the ten commandments, and sealing this covenant with the cultic celebration. Today's scholarly research is more and more inclined to present the old-oriental, especially the Hethite form of covenant,[4] as a formal analogy for God's covenant with Israel. It is encouraging to see that this attempt aims to better understand the relation of the covenant from a biblical-theological point of view, that much more importance is attributed to the covenant as a means of divine action, and that researchers take a much wider view of the biblical texts so that the theologumenon "covenant" is presented in its central position.

By its position and function the Decalogue essentially belongs to God's covenant with Israel, for it marks the way which Israel has to tread in order to fulfill its part in the agreement. Therefore it is not sufficient to see in it only a codification of the natural law.[5]

4. LEVITICUS AND NUMBERS

Here light is shed upon that great complex of law contained in the Pentateuch, which is the source of all traditional law as it kept pace with the changing conditions of daily life. Thus we have a centuries-long process of evolution making law what it is today. From the authoritarian-like formulated type of law (see the Decalogue) we differentiate the casuistically-formed law that was customary outside of Israel.[6]

As demonstrated in Leviticus and Numbers, these collections of laws and regulations reveal a special relation to God in the institution of the cult, in the ordination of high priests, priests, and Levites, and in the construction of the sacred text and the Torah. The most divergent types of familial and social laws and norms were in force. It is believed that these complex laws attained their present form only after the exile, that is, around 500 B.C., which indicates that there were considerable adaptations according to the exigencies of the people of God. The so-called *Holiness Code* of Leviticus 17:27 deserves special mention because it belonged to the Priestly scriptures but certainly worked over ancient material. Whereas Leviticus seems to be exclusive in its legal character, we find Numbers recording various legal ordnances and regulations along with the latest events on Sinai, the migrations of the people as far as the land of Moab. Here the appearance of the pagan seer Balaam is particularly emphasized: he blesses Israel in Yahweh's name instead of cursing it after the command of his king.

5. DEUTERONOMY

The special value of the fifth Book of Moses lies in the style of his great discourse which renews Israel's pact, hints of God's leadership, and obliges the people to obey the law. It also contains Moses' last address and the reports about his death. This book is a distinct layer of the Pentateuch which seems to have come into its own around 600 B.C., probably after its basic formula had been rescued by Levites following the destruction of Samaria (712 B.C.), and brought into the southern kingdom. In its present form it sets down certain prescriptions in a renewed form and gives new theological implications to the essential individual ordinances as well as the complex of law based on the original covenant. It is no exaggeration to consider it the core of the Old Testament.[7] It sketches the features, valid beyond time, of the people joined to God in its distinction, its prerogatives and duties, its risks and its perils; it speaks about God who out of love has chosen this people and tells how this covenant based on the love of God is to be preserved and fixed for all time into a new and lasting cult. Liturgical regulations are clearly outlined, calling for the one legitimate sanctuary, in the geographical sense of Zion (Dt 12). The salvation of God's people depends on its conduct, that is, its fidelity to God, or, in the case of failure, the self-imposed judgment of God (Dt 25). From this viewpoint, Deuteronomy can be called the official book of God's chosen people which imposes on every generation a renewed fidelity to the covenant by its many interpolated "todays." This fact reveals the *essence* of revelation which continuously calls man to the dialogue of salvation with God.

6. DEUTERONOMIC HISTORIOGRAPHY

M. Noth[8] has so designated the books of Joshua, Judges, 1 and 2 Samuel, and 2 Kings because of their basic general theological concept, which concept derives from the elemental demands of Deuteronomy. This fact indicates the high theological ranking of Deuteronomy for the development of Old Testament salvation history and justifies its designation as "the core of the Old Testament." Retrospectively we see the history of the people of Israel with respect to their fidelity or infidelity to the God of the covenant, and a value judgment of their behavior stems from there. The sanctions, described in such detail in Leviticus 26 and especially in Deuteronomy 28, in the case of fidelity to God but also for the failure of Israel, are considered as magnitudes effective through and coming from God in the deuteronomic historiography, in the history of Israel unto the exile. From this comes the unifying basis of the whole work.

7. JOSHUA AND JUDGES

The first part of the book of Joshua sets out to describe the way God fulfilled the promises given to the Fathers, namely, in the gift of land (Jos 21:45). Yahweh himself intercedes in the Holy War[9] when appropriation of the promised land was possible only through military power, which from then on frequently appears as the only means of assuring the existence of the chosen people. What is at stake here is not desire for conquest, but a determination on the part of the people of God to defend every inch of their precious land—and the possibility for Israel to live in union with God according to the tenets of the covenant.

The second part, which tells about the tribes and their settlements, probably mirrors the lists of tribes of a later epoch. The book ends with the assembly at Shechem in which Joshua renews the covenant with God.

To best characterize the Book of Judges it is necessary to see in it the book of absolute theocracy.[10] Here, better than anywhere else, we can discern the events and validity of the deuteronomic schema of history. In spite of bitter experiences and the imminent threatening anarchy among the loosely united tribes, Israel renounced a ruler on earth in favor of their ruler in heaven (Jgs 8:21ff). Judges are the saving figures elected in times of emergency to banish the acute enemy threat; as leaders in the Holy War they save Israel from the hands of their enemies. Gradually, by this rescue, Israel's return is ef-

fected—or rather, becomes the necessary
precondition for its salvation—and thus Israel
turns away from the gods of its neighbors,
especially Baal, and turns again toward its
own God, Yahweh. Such opposite personali-
ties as Gideon and Samson belong with the
rescuers whose charismatic call comes from
God in a time of crisis.

But in no way does this eliminate the danger of apostasy from God the King, nor the
ensuing inner anarchy, nor the incessant
threat from enemies, nor above all the pres-
sure from the Philistines. A good illustration
concerns the last representatives of this epoch,
the high priest Heli, who cannot keep order
in his own home, let alone among his people.
Therefore he and his house are doomed, and
in his place steps Samuel as the last consci-
entious defender of the absolute kingdom of
God.

8. THE BOOKS OF SAMUEL

Samuel finds himself at a turning point in
the history of revelation and shares the trag-
edy of all such figures in similar situations.
His position can be compared with that of
John the Baptist. Against his will and over
against his own fidelity to the absolute God

the King, he must lend his strength to the introduction of a kingdom in Israel.

The defeat of the people by the Philistines and the loss of the Torah through its falling into the hands of the arch enemy were the factors that prepared Israel for the change toward a temporal king in spite of the opposition of Samuel, the last judge. In the first half of 1 Samuel, texts friendly to the kingdom as well as those opposed to it are alternately brought together (8–12).[11]

In comparison to its surroundings, Israel's kingship comes rather late. When it was introduced, it did not resemble the Canaan system but rather that of the states of Amon, Moab, and Edom. But even under the kings the basis for the coalition still lay in the twelve tribes of Israel. In any case Samuel's reluctance and God's reaction point to the fact that, contrary to other states, all authority, even in the terrestrial state, issued from Yahweh: the chosen people are his property and not, as in the near east, that of the ruling king.

In practice, the kingdom in its beginning perhaps hardly differed from the times of the judges: as were the judges, so are the first two kings called by God, anointed by Samuel, and proclaimed king with the applause of the people. The kingdom of Saul remained only an episode because he violated the essence of his calling as a mere representative of God (Sam 1:15). This experience with their first king was to open Israel's eyes to the fact that their kings could not be absolute rulers but only God's stewards. Thus only the kingship of David becomes the decisive factor in the formation of a kingdom in Israel. Already his development guided by God prepares him for his high dignity to be king in the will of God. He not only banished forever the danger from the Philistines, but subjugated also other peoples (Sam 8:14) and thus prepared the way for Israel's growth from the national state to a great power subsequently leading to the establishment, under his successor Solomon, of a central administration after the model of Egypt and a sumptuous court (2 Sam 20:23–26; 1 Kgs). Despite his fault (2 Sam 11ff), David remains the model for the kings of Israel; his person and his manner of conducting the kingship serve as a model in the deuteronomic history for the successors to the throne of Israel. David's transgression, contrary to Saul's guilt, has no direct bearing on his status as God's representative because his type of guilt, though grave as a consequence of human weakness and loss of self control, does not endanger the foundations of theocracy.

Especially worth mentioning is David's concern for the cult. Not only does he establish Jerusalem as the capital city of the realm but also makes Zion the religious center of the people (2 Sam 6). This action is more than a cold political move: it is rather David's way of thinking which subordinates the political to the religious.

According to 2 Samuel 7, David conceives the thought of erecting a temple. Not he himself, but his son, would start this work. According to Nathan's command, the promise is carried to David's dynasty and finds its culmination in Yahweh's acceptance of the current ruler. In this promise to David's dynasty, which is renewed by David's covenant at every coronation, we see the foundation of the kingdom of Israel as God willed it. Since there does not exist in Israel a typical idea of the state, there develops no proper ideology of kingship in the manner of the old oriental kingdom of God. In spite of God's repeated acceptance of each successive ruler, there was no idolatry of kings. Hence the deepest significance of the Israelite kingdom could only lie in the promise that it would become source and soil for the messianic king of salvation. With Zion as the place of worship and the fulfilled promise to the dynasty of David, two points are given for the further development of Old Testament revelation which bare to us and let us realize the messianic and eschatological side of revelation.

The second part of 2 Samuel (13–24) is mostly dedicated to the family history of David. In it, too, we can recognize the deuteronomic tendency: not only the people, but the individual and even the ruler, are judged and their destinies determined according to their fidelity to God.

9. THE BOOK OF KINGS

Only three possessors of the title of king live up to the high expectations according to which the Deuteronomist is ranking them: David, Hezekiah (contemporary of the Prophet Isaiah) and Josiah (contemporary of the Prophet Jeremiah). Already Solomon, who built the first temple in Jerusalem, falls short of the king-ideal in his later years because of his unbridled passion. Under his son the realm becomes divided into the northern kingdom of Israel or Samaria and the southern kingdom of Judah with Jerusalem as its capital. In the North only two small dynasties are subsequently formed: that of Omri lasts forty years, that of Jehu a bare century. With the fall of Samaria in 721 B.C. the northern kingdom is irretrievably lost; the southern kingdom continues to last with the house of David until the fall of Jerusalem in 586 B.C. and the Babylonian exile.

The three rulers mentioned above originate with the dynasty of David. The other kings of the South either do not live up to the Old Testament idea of kingship in everything or they fail completely in their essential task, and in this they are judged according to their attitude toward the worship of Yahweh. In the eyes of the Deuteronomist only those kings rate who are real defenders of the rightful worship of God in the sole place selected by God, Zion in Jerusalem. If a king remains true to God but permits worship in many places "on high," it is valued as a defect in his personality—not to mention the kings who not only permitted but also furthered the worship of the gods of Canaan and those of the neighboring people and who incited this worship in Yahweh's temple in Jerusalem.

In view of this strict evaluation, not one of the kings of the northern kingdom is recognized.

Soon after the political division of the Great Kingdom of David, another takes place in the religious sphere—thus effecting changes in all areas of life. In northern Dan and Bethel three temples are erected in order to block the pilgrimage of Jerusalem—which for the great holy days is obligatory three times a year. It is obvious that this detachment from Jerusalem creates great dangers for the faith. It is true that Yahweh is also worshiped in Dan and Bethel, but under the strictly forbidden and improper symbol of the calf (Ex 32). This type of veneration the prophets deemed idolatry.

In addition, the worship of foreign gods was also gaining wide recognition among the people, especially under the guise of service to Baal, the main god of the native Canaans. Against this apostasy which spread extensively, there rose the great prophets of action, Elijah and Elisha, whose special mission was that of avid defenders in the battle between Baal and Yahweh on behalf of the one and true God. Their entire preoccupation is absorbed by this present struggle (1 Kgs 17–

41

22, 2 Kgs 1–8).

The intensity of the battle against Baal becomes especially apparent in the figure of Elijah who shows many traits similar to those of Moses. Not only the people, but also the household of the king, are susceptible to the worship of Baal, as can be seen in Jezebel, the alien queen and adversary of the prophet. With all due respect to Elijah and his disciple and successor, Elisha, total apostasy of the people is averted and thus a *rest* always remains faithful; the promise of God continues to endure according to which there are "seven thousand who do not bend their knee before Baal and whose mouth has not kissed him" (1 Kgs 19:18). Elijah, for his staunch defense of the concerns of Yahweh, is honored in a special way on the event of his passing from this world (2 Kgs 2). Another thing becomes clear in the appearance of the two prophets of action: that God neither approves of, nor participates in, the separation of the two kingdoms. Elijah and Elisha are active mostly in the northern kingdom. And even later God commands some of the prophets to go there. In the eyes of God, then, the twelve tribes remain the chosen people of Israel in spite of the political separation.

10. THE CHRONOLOGICAL HISTORIOGRAPHY

There are no other books in the Old Testament whose contents are as similar as those of deuteronomic and chronological history. The latter (1 and 2 Paralipomenon, Esdras, and Nehemiah) coincide with the deuteronomic works in both subject matter and time of reporting. Thus arises the question as to what caused Israel after the exile to want to present again the whole course of its complete history—even the Pentateuch is included in its form of listing tribes (1 Paralipomenon 1–9)—and to so present it in a new interpretation. The answer should be sought in the theological idea which stands as a propelling power behind this work. God's salvific action has not yet come to an end even in the exile and the return home. Nor had the development of revelation subsided, but rather reached a new stage of progress which offered different aspects from those of the kingship days and proper forms of state. Hence the task to regard this development in retrospect and trace the historical growth from a different stance in order to interpret the present correctly.

However, it is safe to say that the deuteronomic works are the chief sources for this new type of presentation even though the minor, but not unimportant, nuances and corrections give a new dimension to the whole. Since the old forms of state had vanished in exile and the post-exilic community had been constructed by the forces of religion, it is understandable that these times can be considered as a new phase of theocracy[12] in which all religious movements so far seem to have come to a standstill. Here is an epoch in which, in contrast to the time of Judges, the people attempt to establish a new life under the immediate rule of God. Hence, certain lines of the past are now seen and judged differently, as necessitated by the new interpretation of history and conditioned by the historical development. In addition, the Chronicler seems to oppose the religious outlook of the Samaritans; they were not accepted into the religious community of the repatriates from Babylon, since they were a mixed people consisting of those who were left behind after the Assyrian capture or who were foreign colonists. Since they continued the tradition of the northern kingdom and ultimately recognized only the Pentateuch, this created tensions which led to a new emphasis in the religion of revelation. Thus the Chronicler stresses above all the worship in Jerusalem, celebrated by a hierarchically ordered priesthood constructed on different levels. In this time we see the great evolution of the priesthood with its increase of priestly authority as a symbol of leadership. David, the pivotal figure in 1 Paralipomenon—whose character traits by far outshine those of Solomon—appears less in the sense of Nathan's prophecy (2 Sam 7) as the founder of a dynasty which is promised to endure, but more as a second Moses, as the advocate of law and worship. These interesting traits, however, the Deuteronomist chooses to ignore; on account of his anti-Samaritan tendencies, the Chronicler pays no attention whatsoever to the kings of the northern country. Just as with David, and not unlike the deuteronomic writer, the Chronicler is concerned with the rulers of the house of David as shown mostly in the description of what they did for the rite. Thus the Chronicler succeeds in representing his current times as a legitimate continuation of the great religious tradition of his people and to explain it as such. While the Deuteronomist is preoccupied in measuring the individual rulers of his time against the ideal of David, the Chronicler pays more attention to how the Davidic institution of worship in the post-exilic times represents a true development and accommodation to the present.

Another instance which is important for an understanding of the biblical books is brought out by the new interpretation of revelation history: that not in every case is it possible to testify justly in one attempt. God's action in salvation history is intensive as well as extensive, and so penetrating and all-embracing that it is impossible to contain it in one sole literary presentation. Compare with this the fourfold gospel stories.

11. THE BOOKS OF PARALIPOMENON

These books now enjoy considerable respect, in contrast to a marked devaluation which they experienced around the turn of the century. Even the post-deuteronomic reports credit them with more historical accuracy and fidelity.

After the genealogy tables (1 Par 1–9), the second part (20–29) is extensively concerned with the kingdom of David, especially in its relation to his preoccupation with the cult. From this it becomes understandable that chapters 10–19 give much more detail than that found in the deuteronomic work concerning the construction of the temple in Jerusalem under Solomon. Texts in 2 Paralipomenon 10–36 contain the history of the kings in the southern kingdom until the time of Cyrus' liberation edict.

12. EZRA

The fact that Ezra takes up Cyrus' edict of liberation (538 B.C.) indicates that the chronicle is being continued here. This is followed by reports on the return, with lists; then there is information about the construction of the second temple which succeeds in spite of the interruptions on the part of the Samaritans (1–6). The priest Ezra reconstructs the post-exilic religious community and cleanses it of all mixed marriages (7–10), those contracted between men of Judah and women of foreign nationality.

13. NEHEMIAH

Here is a description of the above continued efforts, of Nehemiah's travels to Jerusalem, as well as of his concern for the city (construction of the walls) and for the population. In Nehemiah 8–10 we learn of the great renewal of the covenant along with the obligations of the people toward the Mosaic law. The last chapters, 11–13, contain measures for increasing the population and for consecrating the city walls, as well as lists of priests and levites.

In the meantime research is more and more inclined toward the belief that the reorganization of community life in Israel through Nehemiah should be dated ahead of Esdras' religious renewal.

II

TOBIT, JUDITH AND ESTHER

These books, though classed with the historical books of the Old Testament according to traditional division, without a doubt merit a special place. It is not so much the historical happenings of the whole people of Israel but rather the individual fates that are characteristic of Israel's situation at certain times in its history. Hence these reports are more than mere narratives since they extract from the happenings an ever-valid instruction for the people of God; or, better put, they allude only loosely to historical events in order to find the right props for their didactic statements. At any rate, the attempts at combining the isolated occurrences of the three books into one single historical picture and to adapt it to the history of the times have so far met with failure. The authors made liberal use of all the happenings in order to construct of them their didactic narratives.

1. TOBIT

After fourteen chapters of this didactic narrative, Tobit attains wealth in the Assyrian captivity. Later, when he performs works of charity to bury the dead, he is stricken with blindness. The Jewess Sarah is in another dilemma since the demon killed seven of her bridegrooms. In answer to the prayer of both, God sends his angel Raphael to accompany the young Tobit on a voyage to recover the deposited money. The angel frees Sarah from her anguish; and she, according to Judaic law, becomes the wife of Tobit and returns his sight to him. When the two who were helped want to thank the angel for his assistance, he reveals himself and disappears.

This narrative is meant to make Israel conscious of the following teaching: God cares about the fate of every individual who is faithful to him, at home as well as abroad, as long as he follows his dictates. Here, too, the demand of Deuteronomy forms the basis of the presentation. In addition, the instruction seems to infer that in difficult situations God sends his angels in assistance. Angels become increasingly important not only in this deutero-canonical book but also in later texts of the prophets (Zachary, Daniel).[1] This stems from the concept of God in the Old Testament and corresponds to it. While God comes very close to man in the beginning, i.e., the "Angel of Yahweh" in the narratives of the patriarchs, God becomes stronger in the course of revelation history seen in transcendence. The space between him and man is bridged by the angels, in whose function rather than essence the authors are interested. Their function is that of harbingers of salvation or judgment of God to men and to transmit prayers and requests from man to God.

2. JUDITH[2]

In exilic as well as post-exilic times Israel gradually came to recognize the fact that there were other powers to fight beyond those of the contemporary world, namely, the *anti-God*—in our words, the Antichrist—who is the enemy of the true God. In order to illustrate this teaching, the sixteen chapters of

51

Judith relate how Nebuchadnezzar equipped an expeditionary force under Holofernes so as to punish the Western people, Judah among them. The Jews are surrounded and in dire straits. Then Judith appears, promises her help, and gets herself into the enemy camp. She succeeds in outwitting and killing the enemy. With this the tables are turned— Judith is acclaimed for her work in that great anguish, but she herself sings a song of praise to the Lord and sacrifices her spoils in the temple as a gift of consecration.

If the Book of Tobit gives prominence to the fate of the individual Jew who is faithful to God, the Book of Judith accents the fate of a whole people. In metahistorical traits, the events which make use of a series of elements from history become an overall, valid instruction for the people of God. In boundless arrogance and impudence Nebuchadnezzar appropriates the name and the power of God. This pseudo-God who wants to bend all the world to his will through the might of his arms is beaten not by a superior or equal might of arms but by the power of true faith. (This narrative indeed is based on the attack of the Assyrians, the first part of which Isaiah reports.) The true God rescues his weak, insignificant people through the power of a woman. By this God proclaims to the world that he can freely toss about even the highest human might and that he can rescue his people and deliver them even from the most desperate situation (1 Cr 27). Nebuchadnezzar symbolizes the ever-present enemy of the Kingdom of God and in his type is revealed the fact that the Kingdom of God on earth will always encounter its enemies but that it can endure under the protection of God if it remains faithful to him. The narrative is sometimes couched in apocryphal terms.

3. ESTHER

It can be assumed that the historical background in the ten chapters which compose the Book of Esther is much stronger than that in the two preceding works. But this does not mean that Esther is a historical work which can be controlled and traced in all its details.

The king of Persia gains the Jewess Esther for his wife. Haman, the king's vesier, decides on the destruction of the Jews. Following her uncle's advice, Esther twice seeks out the king. Thus she succeeds in sparing her people from the disaster which is threatening them.

In memory of this rescue the feast of Purim
is still being celebrated.

Esther is the book of the persecuted and
suffering Jewish people. If the people per-
severe in faith, they will always suffer pain
and persecution from the hands of God's
worldly enemies but with God's help will
overcome all aggravations and will be sup-
ported by him.

4. RUTH

The date of the four chapters which comprise this little book has to be a rather late
one. Written in masterful Hebrew, it was
prized especially because of its poetic quali-
ties; its narrative looks back upon an ancient
tradition. We hear that Elimelech of Bethle-
hem, on account of a famine, emigrated with
his family to Moab. There his two sons marry
Moabite wives. One of the daughters-in-law,
Ruth, returns home with her mother-in-law,
becomes the wife of Booz, and thus enters the
line of descendants of the house of David
and Jesus.

There is still discussion as to whether the
book was written in order to glorify the royal
family of David or to protest against the marriage laws of Esdras, who has marriages with

foreign women dissolved even though they are, as in the case of Ruth, "converts." But possibly the book wants to present belief in retribution and thus would somehow come closer to Job.

5. THE BOOKS OF THE MACCABEES

Having come to us only in the Greek language, these two books tell about the war of liberation which the Jews waged against the Seleucids, especially against Antiochus IV.

1 Maccabees related in sixteen chapters the foundation and destruction of the kingdom of Alexander, the revolt of Judas Maccabee under Mattathias (166 B.C.) against the godless Antiochus; the wars of liberation of the sons of Judas under whose reign the temple is reconsecrated in 165 B.C.; and the reign of Jonathan and Simon the high priest until the ascension to the throne of John Hyrcanus I in 135 B.C.

In fifteen chapters 2 Maccabees contains individual descriptions of the revolt of the Maccabees, for instance, the letters of the Jews in Palestine to Egypt; Heliodorus' attack on the temple treasure; the martyr deaths of the seven brothers; the heroic deeds of Judas; the death of the nefarious Antiochus;

and the inauguration of the feast for the purification of the temple.

From a theological point of view, the theme of these two books is the restoration of theocracy in Israel, more after the model of Judges than the post-exilic renewal of this institution. The messianic expectation, which had its foundation in the dynasty of David, is directed to the Hasmoneans and is realized in them. According to 2 Maccabees especially, the eschatological expectation of the present is contained in this "Old Testament Church" similar to the time of Judges, only at a much more advanced stage of revelation. Fidelity to law and the tradition of the fathers are considered the norm and rule for a renewed theocracy.[3]

III

THE DIDACTIC WRITINGS

The chronistic work of history, in contrast to the deuteronomic, had its origin in the new interpretation of Israel's history so as to bring it up to the exigencies of the post-exilic times. In general, we could designate the books treated here as "seat in life," since, under revelation, they attempt to explain new complexes and difficulties that were emerging in Israel's life with its God. This means that an attempt was made to explicate a new interpretation—or even a first interpretation—of such problems which, until then, had not been urgent but have turned up as problematic later in the course of history. The goal here is to master the whole breadth of life in its various dimensions and to understand it from the aspect of its covenant with God. To this end serve the experiences of every-day life and the reflections aimed at practical life.

1. JOB

The frame of this book which comprises forty-two chapters is the fate of a righteous non-Israelite named Job (Ezk 14:14, 20): his piety, his fortune, his trial and temptation by Satan, his misfortune, and finally, in the end, the restoration of his former state of happiness and prosperity. The main part contains the three speeches of his three friends who feel that his plight can only be due to some secret guilt; thus they master the problem of misery in the world. All he has left is to plead his innocence until God in a theophany reveals to him that the human mind cannot probe the depth of creation's secrets nor the omniscience of his plan with men and their sufferings. God thus reaffirms Job's innocence and refutes the friends' contention that suffering is necessarily a consequence of sin.

From the literary critic's point, the authenticity of the wisdom speech (chap. 28) and Elihu's speeches, (chap. 32–37) is doubtful.

In its literary genre this book represents a

great work of art which deserves to be cited among the famed monuments of world literature. It specifically discusses the problem of the suffering of innocents. This is very skillfully based on the strict rules of speech and counterspeech. The incomprenhensible fate of the noble Job who loses his fortune as well as all his children and who is afflicted with a loathsome disease begins a debatable question which has been tormenting men of all times in an attempt to find a satisfactory answer.

The view of the Israelites in the post-exilic epoch is expressed in the speeches of the three friends: the truly fine man's fate on earth will be a good one, and that of the sinner will be bad. Since the divine rule on earth seems to uphold the principle of just retribution, the consequences which the friends deduct from Job's case are formulated in this way: because Job has met with great misfortune he necessarily must be guilty, at least in secret, and is indeed a sinner. Hence what more can Job do but proclaim his innocence; he does not see any reason for his sufferings but nevertheless cannot break his rock-like confidence in God. Another anonymous wisdom teacher finds no solution until God himself in a theophany answers the tormenting question concerning suffering. By God's not making it any clearer, it is apparent that the final insight into his universal rule will always be denied to man. God thus refers Job to the wonders of creation which remain unintelligible to man. If man is unable to understand God's secrets in nature, how much less can he understand God's plan for man in ruling the world as he measures out to man fortune and misfortune, joy and suffering, in secret counsel without becoming unjust? Nor does the New Testament give a satisfactory solution to this question but rather commands us to overcome suffering by the belief in the glory to come (Rm 8:18). Thus, for Job as well as for those in the gospels, suffering remains a goad and incitement on the path to perfection. As proof of his innocence, Job is permitted to offer prayers for his nonunderstanding friends and with this act achieves a role of mediator like that of Abraham and Moses.

2. PSALMS

This collection of one hundred and fifty songs—representing one of the most important books of Holy Scripture and the whole world literature—is divided, similar to the

Pentateuch, into five books: 1–41; 42–72; 73–89; 90–106; 107–150. The present-day arrangement and division of the psalms, which show a definitive resemblance to the five books of Moses,[1] can be understood in their relation to the synagogue worship. The themes of the psalms touch nearly all the questions and problems of the Old Testament.

Modern research, especially since Gunkel,[2] is concerned with the different categories of psalms and their position in life, with the tradition of the psalms until they reached their present form, and with the numerous theological problems contained in them, to name only a few. A new direction in the research of comparative religion—the "myth and ritual" school and the Scandinavian psalm research triggered by it, especially the school of Uppsala—has found in this work stimulation and suggestions for their specially formed understanding of the Old Testament. The following categories today are widely recognized: hymns, songs of mourning, hymns of thanksgiving, psalms of supplication, psalms for pilgrimages, psalms for processions, songs of kings, didactic psalms, "messianic" psalms, and others.

Without a doubt the Psalter occupies a

special place in the books of the Old Testament, since the psalms permit unique insights into the inner structure of revelation. The Psalter testifies to the fact that revelation is not acted out as a monologue by God but that God has found a partner in his chosen people whom he is drawing into the development of revelation. Just as, according to our understanding of inspiration, God and the hagiographers together share in the composition of Holy Scriptures, thus the chosen people is God's partner in revelation and elsewhere. Revelation is experienced as a dialogue. Not only does God act and speak regarding the people, but Israel also acts and speaks (see Ex 19:8 where the people respond collectively that they will do everything the Lord has said). Like no other biblical book, the Psalms proclaim the people's role in revelation—their readiness for dialogue and their responses to God. This interaction is demonstrated clearly by certain corresponding examples: Act of creation and creation proper, Gn 1—Ps 102 (103); man, Gn 1:26ff, 2—Ps 8. God's sanctity, Is 6—Ps 99 (98); man, Gn 1:26ff, 2—Ps 8. The parting of the sea, Ex 13–15—Ps 66 (65). Praise of the God of the Covenant, Ex 19–24

—Ps 97 (96). From Egypt to the promised land, Ps 114 (113A). From the time of the patriarchs to the acquiring of lands, Ps 105 (104). God's work of salvation in Zion, 2 Sam 6—Ps 48 (47). The New Covenant, Jer 31:31–34, Ezk 36:24–28—Ps 51 (50), 12ff. The Messiah as King, Is 9:1–6, 2:1–5, Mi 5:1–4—Ps 2, 72 (71), 110 (109). The Messiah as Sufferer, Is 53—Ps 22 (21).

It is only natural that there is no exact textual concordance between the texts cited. The main themes are taken up in the psalms by the people of God singing hymns of praise, but interpreted anew into an expanding revelation with ever fuller and more relevant meanings. Secondly, the psalms point out that Israel's foremost and noblest task—the very reason for its singular existence—rests in its worship of God. It bespeaks Israel's selection over all the surrounding peoples: Israel has been chosen particularly so as to sing God's praises. It is precisely in the Chronicles that we learn about this praise of God in the mouths of the people or those of the Levites who are specially appointed to do so, and this aspect of worship may well have influenced the present-day arrangement of the songs in the Psalter.[3] Not without reason has it been affirmed that Nehemiah 8:1–6 contains a model for the synagogue worship that rose alongside the temple worship in post-exilic times. Since the sacrificial worship remained restricted to the temple, we have here a purely liturgical form that might be comparable to our Introit of the Mass. We can distinguish the following parts in it: The reading of the corresponding Pentateuch pericope. The five books of Moses are distributed to each Sabbath of the year during a span of three years (with special pericopes designated for feast days). Then follows the corresponding psalm (probably sung by the congregation). The ordering of the psalm with the lessons of the Pentateuch is linked to the principal figure of the lessons, which, however, does not represent the main theme as we conceive it. If we go through the Psalter in this way, we recognize the underlying order principle, not apparent until today, consisting in the very linking of psalms and Pentateuch lessons.

Thus we may assume with a certain degree of assurance that the Psalter received its present-day form in the epoch of the reestablishment of the post-exilic community under

Esdras and Nehemiah. In addition, its use in the synagogue worship indicates a certain order demanded by the different complexes of the Pentateuch and brings them close together, which of course explains why the final redaction of the individual biblical books requires a broader view than that of simply praising God. Mowinckel and Weiser[4] have especially pointed out this fact.

3. PROVERBS

Contemporary theological discussions[5] recognize more and more that wisdom literature has a long history, the individual phases of which, however, cannot be traced any longer due to the lack of traditional historical indications. Stimulated by the differing legal complexes of the Pentateuch, the expressions of wisdom were written down and first collected during the times of Solomon. He established a school for scribes in Jerusalem and took up relations with the outside world. In Egypt and Mesopotamia such proverbs of wisdom had long since been known as the sum of well-digested life experience. The Book of Kings itself (1 Kgs 5) praises the outstanding wisdom of Solomon; in Israel the exercise of this literary genre and the first known collection of proverbs will always be connected with his name.

The book contains thirty-one chapters of different groups of proverbs. First we have Solomon's collection (1–9) which extol the praise of wisdom. But in the main the poet warns his readers, as does the teacher his pupil, of the manifold dangers and vices, especially adultery. As this part, which may be of a later date, is in the form of a prologue, chapters 10–22 represent the principal part of the book. In small proverbs and maxims well-proven experiences of wisdom are represented. Chapters 23–31 contain smaller collections and terminate in the praise of the ideal wife.

What may be called Semitic humanism can best be traced in the Book of Proverbs, which has grown to its present extent from small beginnings and core representations. It is thus a collection of various small details which are concerned with different phases of life and different professions and which indicate rules and regulations for proper behavior. In the background of these stands *Wisdom* which, according to Psalm 1, man uses to meditate about revelation and which man acquires in the course of his long life. A real teacher of wisdom, in addition, is one who helps young men find insights and experiences. The teachings of the book are thoroughly imbued, so to say, with God's revelation as it is contained especially in the Pentateuch. The wisdom literature which sometimes borrows from old oriental models explains how revelation can be brought down to human understanding and knowledge and how "wisdom" resulting from it is apt to guide the life of man believing in revelation and to help him master it.

4. ECCLESIASTES

Behind this equivocal term is hidden an experienced teacher of wisdom who is presenting his teachings not in the temple but in the circle of his disciples. We can hardly discover a logical order of procedure in the twelve chapters of this book. The entire content of these writings is constantly showing ever-changing aspects all of which, however, are aimed at one central thesis: "Everything is vain." Finally, the author comes to the conclusion that moderate enjoyment of life during youth is what remains most desirable on earth. For man is denied the deeper insight into the essence of things and has to answer above all to God's judgment.

The preacher, caller *kohelet* in Hebrew, can be compared to Job. The book confronts the exegete with considerable difficulties and could lead exegesis into extreme ways. The book has been called "the quintessence of piety," but also "the quintessence of pessimism." Certainly both, but especially the latter, are quite exaggerated. In reality this book, which according to its language must be dated in the late post-exilic epoch, expresses a deep knowledge of life and has already recognized that all things on earth possess only restricted value. God alone lives forever. Yet he does not act in the manner of men, and a glimpse into his wisdom is denied us. Thus, true wisdom of man is to recognize God's action everywhere, to constantly obey his commands, and to use earthly goods so that man in everything he does can pass muster before God's judgment.

The manner of speaking and the line of thought in Ecclesiastes frequently strike us as extremely modern and often as most relevant to modern life. He could be considered the "existential" philosopher of the Bible.

5. SONG OF SONGS[6]

This is a collection of songs contained in eight chapters, the theme of which is marital love. Exegetes are still in doubt as to the number of songs and paragraphs as well as to the exact nature of the love that is described, that is, whether it is between a betrothed or married couple. There is a profound candor in these lyrics, which is typical of the oriental mentality. Though erotic throughout, the language is neither obscene nor offensive in its representation of the type of love the couple has for each other. The songs dwell on the theme of deep human love.

Certainly no other book in all of the Old Testament Canon is as widely argued as is the Song of Songs. Tradition—the Jewish included—has mainly interpreted it in a symbolic way. Recently modern Catholic scholarship is more and more leaning toward an interpretation that sees in the Songs a deeper understanding of conjugal love, which being founded in God has always occupied a high ranking in the Old Testament. But it is more reasonable to assume that the author or collector of these old love songs of post-exilic times conferred a deeper sense to them,

namely, that of typologically forming the
Song of Songs according to God's love for his
people. This is borne out by the fact that in
the post-exilic epoch the people lived in the
true spirit of the prophets and in a renewed
religious atmosphere and the fact that the
Canticle of Canticles was to become the feast-
roll for the passover feast.

The prophets Ezekiel, Hosea, and Jeremiah
present this same relationship of God to his
chosen people under the guise of the nuptial
pact. This deeper sense at the same time
parallels the closest human relationship with
the ineffable and selfless love of God. Thus
the earthly love extolled in these poems is
elevated to the high plane of the incompre-
hensible love of God for his people. The
sentiments in the Song of Songs reach out to
the New Testament where they fittingly express the relationship of Christ to his bride,
the Church—that mystical union of love between Christ and man. In general, this pro-
jection into the New Testament belongs with
the most significant theological contributions
of the Old Testament writings.

6. WISDOM

This deutero-canonical book of sixteen

chapters enjoyed a great reputation in the ancient Church. The praises of wisdom are sung because it is the cause of blessings. The history of Israel, and especially its exodus, is shown as an example.

Factually we are confronted here with the attempt to coordinate the achievements of Greek philosophy with revelation. From another viewpoint, wisdom is treated like a person who, not as a mere force, stands next to God. Virtues are likewise discussed. Above all it should be stressed that in this rather late book belief in personal immortality is clearly taught. Thereby the book stands on the same idea level with Deuteronomy 12:1–3.

7. SIRACH

In contrast to the Book of Wisdom which in a certain sense is open toward the Greek world of ideas, Sirach, consisting of fifty-one chapters, tries to praise Israel's own tradition. There are similarities to the "categories" in Proverbs as well as reminiscences of psalmody. Its contents recapitulate the great past of Israel and tell of the essence and value of wisdom, of God's position as creator, of the relation of wisdom to the Mosaic law; the book also includes a whole series of rules for a good life and presents teachings on virtue. Finally, in the "Praise of the Fathers" Israel's history is demonstrated again through the example of the leaders chosen by God, and the overwhelming importance of revelation history is respectfully acknowledged. Sirach is much like the Book of Wisdom and has leanings toward the Book of Proverbs. In either case wisdom is made to feature in all the areas of life itself. The same zones of danger, yet in different ways, are pointed out, and these continue to create ever new dangers and temptations in life. In contrast to the Book of Wisdom, Sirach in its background denotes a sharp departure from the often overly powerful influence of Greek thought, which brings with it the danger of turning away from one's own precious treasure of revelation or of watering it down because of overexposure to a foreign world of ideas. Thus we can recognize in the Book of Sirach a deliberate regression to the Mosaic law and a thorough normalization of its statements. Therefore it is not unusual that the book should add the "Praise of the Fathers" in the end, thus turning the faithful toward the glorious, God-directed past of their own people.

Through the wisdom literature the post-exilic faithful establish themselves in their practice of the Mosaic law and in the revelation itself. It becomes a rule of life in their teachings and the norm of life for the post-exilic people of God—or at least for the best of them, for "the holy remnant" for "the peaceful of the land," who remain true to God and take his promises seriously.

IV

PROPHETS

In contrast to the more narrow limitations of the Jewish canon we deal here with the so-called scriptural prophets who according to St. Augustine are divided into major and minor ones.

The very fact that the Jewish canon includes the Prophets among its historical books —with the sole exception of the Pentateuch— is a good indication that the term "prophet" needs a somewhat fuller explanation.

All we can say about the term is that present-day language usage is not adequate enough to express completely what the Bible originally meant by "prophet." The generally accepted notion of prophet is that of "seer." But this is only one side, and not even the most important, of a biblical prophet. In Scripture the terminology embraces a meaning by far more extensive: a prophet is one who openly and responsibly speaks in the name of God. Thus Abraham and Moses are called prophets. In the case of Abraham,[1] therefore, to be a prophet is not a matter of simply representing God, or of worthily revealing God's word, but rather one of serving as God's mediator (Gn 20:7). Since the Old Testament concept of prophet is so deeply rooted in the prophet's being the recipient of divine revelation, it is therefore not surprising that the prophetic canon in the Jewish order is numerically greater than ours. In general, the number of prophets called by God is much greater than we might surmise from the biblical books named after them. There are many among them who have not come down in the tradition of authors, for instance Nathan, a prophet at the time of David. In Saul we read of communities of prophets (1 Sam 19:10) ; Elijah and Elisha are heads of schools for prophets (2 Kgs 2:15). All through revelation history God calls prophets as harbingers and executors of his will. The two centuries before the Babylonian captivity are considered the classical age of prophets. Yahweh calls on the prophets in the recurring critical points of this historical epoch when the kings frequently neglect their religious calling by wanting to take an undue active part in contemporary politics or resort to apostasy by worshiping Baal. The task of prophets was to divert the threatening and self-inflicted downfall of Israel, to arrest the headlong rush toward destruction by their unique insights and the power of God's word, and thus to preserve in Israel the form of an individual state. But in spite of all the warnings and admonitions, the people of Israel shun reform.

But the prophets, beyond stressing the contemporary theme, announce in a special way the coming kingdom of God. In the present, God's kingdom has not been realized according to his promise because of the constant failures of the chosen people. Hence, from the current and newly experienced failure of the present, the prophets shift their outlook to the future, sometimes with tremendous dynamics, to that great salvific work which will fulfill the promises of God. The prophets, as we see, always stand by God in the times of crisis in Israel's history and remain his chosen faithful mediators. We want to remind of the word of Am 3:7: "Indeed the Lord God does nothing without revealing his plan to his servants, the prophets." They translate the content of the salvation expectancy according to the progress of revelation and the exigencies of their times. They exhort the faithful and prod them never to become lax here and now, but to keep their hearts and minds open for the great future event of salvation which God, in unshakable fidelity, will effect in the fullness of time through his anointed.

It is especially in the prophets that we can discern the difference between the oriental religions of nature and the religion of revelation formed through the history of Israel.[2] In the natural religions the main accent is placed on the concrete course of the year, with rites that exhaust themselves in expressing, often through magical practices, the course of nature and the well-being and growth of men and animals for the coming year—and making certain the assistance of the godhead in this restricted sphere of nature. In the religion of revelation on the contrary, this sphere of nature is merely the instrument through which God, acting and intervening in the history of man, can keep man close to himself. The relation of God with man in a freely entered covenant, founded on God's initiative, transcends the natural cycle and is aimed at the future to which the historical movement is progressing, triggered by revelation. Thus the course it takes is linear in spite of all the detours and errors, not cyclic and regressive, but rather spirally directed toward the expectation of the future salvific action of God.

1. ISAIAH

The most extensive and significant prophetic work of the Old Testament is doubtless the Book of Isaiah. Hyronymus called this prophet the "Evangelist of the Old Testament." A prophet by this name appears in the southern kingdom about 738 to 800 B.C., but even a very superficial reading reveals that this book is not of one redaction and as a whole could not have originated in the times of the prophet.

The first part, 1–39, is attributed to the Prophet Isaiah himself in its chief, fundamental thesis; it is also safe to assume as later additions the great Isaiah-Apocalypse, 24–27, as well as the historical events of the times of King Hezekiah (36–39; see also 2 Kgs 18f).

Here as everywhere in the prophetic texts a knowledge of the historical background is of utmost importance for understanding the whole. Along with prophecies of threat against Israel this book contains above all those concerning Emmanual (7–12) with the promise of messianic King of Peace. With the imagery of the present ruler of the house of David, the Prophet sketches the expected one who fulfills the great promises and thus more than satisfies the figure of a king in 2 Samuel 7. This prefigured king of salvation is portrayed against the background of the Assyrian invasion through which the mortal powers appear on the scene—taken into service by God, it is true, but a prey to judgment because of their own guilt and hybris. This is followed by threatening utterances against foreign peoples and cities (13–23). After the great apocalyptic book of the great misery, judgment and rescue of Jerusalem follow.

It is rather difficult to render a clear line of thought all through the prophetic books. The themes vary throughout and cover the whole gamut of biblical theology in the warnings and salvation utterances. Already in the vision when Isaiah is called, Yahweh appears as the King of the World who exercises his uni-

versal kingship on an ethical basis, erects a
sign of his revelation in Israel and Jerusalem,
and expects in faith man's answer to the
covenant. Revelation is directed toward an
important act of salvation in the future which
will be realized in the person of the expected
one. It focuses toward fulfillment in the
eschatological time after a pause in the present time. But to achieve this Israel must
endure a test of faith insofar as the enemy
powers which go to war against Israel are concerned. In the end they, too, will be saved,
thanks to Israel's mediation (2:19), and this
becomes the goal of history after the universal
judgment and consequently has a close connection with God (24–27).

Even though chapters 40–55 resemble in
style and form those of the first part of the
book, the situations of the prophet who speaks
and of the people he addresses have notice-
ably changed. In this second part the Babylonian exiles who are addressed find solace
in it one hundred and fifty years after the
prophet Isaiah. These are the easily discern-
ible additions: 42:1–7; 49:1–9; 50:4–9;
52:13–53; twelve of them are called the
"Servant Songs." Modern exegetes are still
debating whether or not Isaiah is actually the

writer of the second part. If an unknown author has to be acknowledged, it is indeed true to say that the Servant Songs are very skillfully fitted into the overall complex.

In the second part, Yahweh appears more as the universal ruler of the world. Here the expected eschatological salvation is highly accented and is separated, together with the whole revealed faith, from any close connection with that earthly kingdom of Israel which disappeared in exile; rather the new approach in the second part is ordered to the essential, religious realm which transcends the earthly one. The interpretation of the Servant Songs poses great problems of interpretation.[3] Behind the figure in question the exegete sees either the future task of the whole people faithful to God or that of an outstanding religious personality. But this expresses only a certain tension detected in the songs. Another ambiguity is sensed in the polarity within the songs of the two concepts of king and prophet. The texts do not exactly confirm whether this "servant of God" is meant to be a royal figure as is hinted by the terminology, or if it is not perhaps a prophet, and, if so, is it right to class him with Moses, Jeremiah, and others. The third point of tension adds another question: Is it really a contemporary figure, as it strongly appears to be, or does the writer have in mind the announcement of an eschatological figure, an assumption more in line with the overall tone of the whole. In spite of all the nebulous, minute details the songs show a progressive individual tendency; they point to an unknown servant of God who, rooted in the world of God and coming from it, faces a dual prophetic task: he must renew God's covenant wtih Israel and in his missionary guise transmit to the pagans the light of revealed religion. With this task which, basically, is also the selective task of all of Israel, and thus the collective element of all the songs, the servant of Yahweh surpasses every historical figure of the chosen people, both king and prophet, and therefore should be determined as the greatest figure of salvation for the future, that is, a royal figure, a messianic figure. While Israel falls short of its prophetic mission, this *servant* will fulfill his task in a unique way. This uniqueness becomes apparent especially in the representative atoning death of the servant for the sins "of the many," a fact which is alien to the Old Testament and is not accepted in spite of Moses' offer (Ex 32, 32f) but will be realized only in Christ.

Seen from this point of view, the Servant Songs belong to the most significant and most beautiful texts of the Old Testament. They were able to console the people in exile, to recall to them the power of revelation, and to enable them to face the future with confidence.

When it is assumed, as is generally the case today, that these chapters (Is 40–55) belong to the time of exile and presuppose an unknown author and not the prophet who lived a hundred and fifty years earlier, the question remains as to why these later chapters do not form a separate book but are added to Isaiah. It can be surmised that the reason lies in the possibility that a varied authorship of the new part had felt obligated to the prophet Isaiah. Similar to Jesus, the great prophets probably assembled disciples around themselves who passed on the words of their masters and interpreted them anew from generation to generation. The fact that Isaiah's influence was so far-reaching is a sign of the dynamic quality of his prophetic work. The disciples who carried on the tradition seem to disappear into anonymity for a long span of time and attribute to their master all that they have written.

There could also be new avenues of interpretation leading to the third part, 56–66. Here we have a collection of diverse texts that expose a post-exilic point of view. The surviving circle of the prophet's disciples illumine this situation spiritually and interpret it accordingly.

2. JEREMIAH

Born of a small, priestly family Jeremiah sought to live a modest, quiet life in the midst of his own kin. But he is pulled away from this serenity by God himself and against his will is cast into the limelight to proclaim to the people merciless words of judgment. He was born supposedly in 650 B.C. and in 626 called to the service of prophet. During the span of his career there were three concrete causes in the religious and political situation of his people that had influenced his oracles. After 626 he concerns himself with the unity of worship as laid down in Deuteronomy, which means that he saw to it that Yahweh should legitimately be worshiped only in Zion. From his remaining silent after the reform of Josiah in 621, it is obvious that he accomplished his purpose. Not before 605, under King Jehoiakim, does he again see a reason to appear as a prophet. He warns against underestimating the might of Babylon and urges the recognition of Nebuchadnezzar as a ruler who receives the call and the limits of his power from God. Once more before the fall of Jerusalem in 586 Jeremiah appears with an oracle in order to wend off the impending disaster, but to no avail. Rebels finally kidnap him, and after the catastrophe he chose the offer of the Babylonian king to remain in his country; he was then forcibly taken to Egypt where all traces of him were lost.

As to the literary history of this book we can distinguish certain layers of compilation. First, the original scroll, that is, the words of the prophet as his servant, Baruch, took them down. Following the destruction of the early scroll, Jeremiah dictates another to his servant Baruch, which fact is made clear in chapter 36; the deposit of the prior phases of his prophetic work can be found in chapters 2–20. Baruch had embellished the original scroll with additional discourses and biographical texts which reach as far as the departure for Egypt in 585 B.C. Finally, the manuscript in this form was submitted to careful deuteronomic redaction by the disciples of the prophet during the Babylonian exile. In the course of this process the book received its present format of fifty-two chapters. During this final stage the book came to resemble the deuteronomic hagiography by prominently featuring the axiom of deuteronomic history and construction. It may be assumed that the same forces which gave the deuteronomic history its final shape were also active in the final redaction of this book.

Chapters 26–35 contain the prophecies of salvation, 36–45 the historical reports, 46–51 the threatening speeches against peoples. We should add here that the Septuagint translated another shortened basic text.

Not only do we recognize in the figure of Jeremiah the burden of his call from God—which vocation fills his entire life—but also the ravages of the critical times in which he lived. These are the turbulent decades before the greatest catastrophe in Israel's history in which Jeremiah is sent by God to exhort the people and hold them back from their obstinate headlong rush to perdition. But he must watch his prophetic words go unheeded by most of them, and he is helpless to stop the inexorable fate in spite of his urgent appeals.

Just as Cyrus, the king of Persia, is honored in Deutero-Isaiah for his significant role in the renewal of the religious community, Jeremiah sees in the Babylonian king Nebuchadnezzar the world ruler after God's will: God has endowed him with worldly power, God uses him as a scourge for his people, and God also sets the limits for the spread and the duration of his power. These expressions clearly reveal Jeremiah's theological conviction that God is the ruler of the world as such, that he delegates worldly power inside and outside of Israel, and that consequently the history of his people is enmeshed with the course of world history which is regulated by God.

In view of this close relationship of ideas with Deuteronomy and the deuteronomic hagiography, we need not be surprised that the Covenant of Israel with God plays a decisive role. Deuteronomy as the center of the Old Testament is the book of the people of God and therefore the book of the covenant of Mount Sinai. Against the background of the catastrophe of 586, Jeremiah gives birth to the idea of a coming New and Eternal Covenant (31, 32) which will link the new

Israel closer to God than will the old covenant of Mount Sinai which was broken so frequently. It is not because the old covenant has failed its task, but because Israel has failed its, that the future will see a New Covenant. In the New the laws will be brought even closer to the people: these new laws will be engraved directly into the changed hearts of the covenant partner, so that Israel will freely cleave to God. In its essence and its goals the New Covenant is founded on the Covenant of Mount Sinai and continues the development of revelation. Jeremiah has achieved lasting prominence with this prophecy, for it projects directly into the salvific action of Jesus (see Lk 22, 20; 1 Cor 2:25).

3. LAMENTATIONS

The subject of these five very skillfully constructed songs attributed to Jeremiah deals with the destruction of the temple by Nebuchadnezzar. The miseries of the besieged city, the punishment and sufferings of the people, and their humiliations are detailed in the lamentations before God. At the same time the prayer for the punishment of the evildoers, especially of the archenemy Edom, is proffered. The last song terminates in a plea to God not to forget and abandon his people, but to grant it a new future.

This little book, according to modern critics, did not originate in Jeremiah but probably in circles which were close to the Holy of Holies. It may have been composed shortly after the destruction of the temple in 586 B.C. Or rather, the different songs without literary affinity, but alike in theme, were probably assembled about that time.

4. BARUCH

This little book which is attributed to the disciple and confidant of the Prophet Jeremiah has come down to us only in Greek. It contains five chapters, three of them completely different single texts: a prayer of atonement, a praise of wisdom, then lamentations and consolations. The Vulgate adds in the form of a sixth chapter the letter of Jeremiah against idolatry in which he exposes the idols and their worshipers to ridicule; there are paragraphs of seventy-two verses. Hyronymus has labeled this letter post-exilic, a concept which has been generally accepted. The book as a whole received its present shape only in late post-exilic times.

5. EZEKIEL

These forty-eight chapters are very well organized, as manifested by the three main sections. Ezekiel's call to the task of prophet (1–3) induces three utterances against Juda and Jerusalem. The second part (25–32) contains prophecies of threats against the neighboring pagan nations similar to those we find in Isaiah and Jeremiah. The third part is a book of consolation with promises pertaining to the reconstruction of Jerusalem (33–48). At first we hear about preparations for the time of salvation in the renewal of the nation toward a new existence (37). This time of salvation will be preceded by a last, extremely vehement attack of the enemy Gog from Magog (38f). After that the prophet as priest examines the new laws of the coming kingdom of God and unfolds before us the plans of the temple for the time of salvation, describing the new worship in the Holy City.

When we read Ezekiel carefully, it becomes quite clear that this gigantic work could not possibly have arisen overnight but necessarily represents the sum of prophetic activity over one or more decades, from about 595 to 580 B.C., in Babylon. Yet this great prophetic book more than any other carries the individual stamp of the prophet himself. Even if the work was subjected to an "interpretive editing" (Dreissler), the traces of the prophet are unequivocal.

Ezekiel because of his priestly background and the traditions of his people, shows evidence of this in his linguistic style—versatile, picturesque, sometimes even drastic. While the audio and the visual are well balanced in Isaiah and Jeremiah—leaning toward the audio in Jeremiah—the visual trait is outstanding in Ezekiel.

As one of those forced to depart in 597 B.C., he admonishes those who remained at home, as did Jeremiah, to yield to the rule of Babylon. He deplores the continued defection of the people and in chapter 16, for example, traces a meaningful comparison between married life and the love of God for his people—the incident of the two prostitute sisters (Judah and Samaria). Continuing Jeremiah's thought, he shifts the responsibility from the people as a whole to the individual (18). Until now the whole people was addressed as receiver of revelation directly from God, and the individual was only a member of this whole people. But since the catastrophe of 586 and the disappearance of the people as a national unit and might, a new partner in the dialogue with God had to be approached by the prophets in continuation of revelation.

Thus, through Ezekiel, through his well understood religious individualism, a further stage in universal religious development is encountered. The basic structure, so to say, for the New Covenant is prophesied by Ezekiel by way of a complete change of heart in man, one symbolizing a complete renewal of man. Together with Jeremiah and Deutero-Isaiah, Ezekiel—through his detailed and concrete planning and layout for the Holy of Holies, for the priesthood, and for worship—belongs with the prophets who look beyond the catastrophe of their people by continuing the development of revelation and by boldly representing the time of salvation still to come as the goal of salvation history guided by God.

6. DANIEL

In the Christian concept Daniel belongs with the four great prophets. In the Jewish canon he appears among the wisdom writings, probably because at the time when the book which is named after him originated, the canon of prophets was already finished. It is hard to discern if the Daniel mentioned in Ezekiel 14:20 with Noah and Job can be identified with the title figure of this book. If we gather the data available for the life of Daniel, we find that he was born about 620 B.C. and was still alive under the Persian King Cyrus in 540, which would make him 80 years old. These biographical sources however do not furnish enough grounds to establish him as the originator of this book.

The first part of the narrative (1–6) tells the story of how Daniel and his friends came to the court of Babylon. Daniel interprets Nebuchadnezzar's dream; his friends are thrown into the fiery furnace. The banquet of Belteshazzar and Daniel's rescue from the lions' den are included here. The second part acquaints us with Daniel's visions of the four worldly kingdoms and the kingdom of God in messianic times, the most important of which portray the visions of the son of man and the Seventy-Weeks' Prophesy (9). The so-called deutero-canonical appendix, which comes down to us only in Greek, contains chapters 13 and 14 with the story of the virtuous Susanna, the trickery at Bel's worship, and the description of Daniel killing the dragon.

One of the many problems posed by this book lies in the language barriers: 1,1–2; 4; 8–12 are in Hebrew, 2:4–7 Aramaic, 13 Greek. In addition there is a series of words borrowed from the Persian. In contrast to other accounts of the prophets, the author says nothing about his call to service nor does he have the task of addressing the people directly and explaining God's salvation or judgment to them. Rather, these apocalyptic reports present the goals and values of history as well as the function and importance of the people of God and its particular calling within the framework of world history.

In the past exegetes have taken great care to interpret correctly the historical survey of this book which is rather nebulous in its details. We might note here that in spite of repeated efforts, an exact interpretation of the historical background of the Near East will never be achieved. An example would be chapter 2 with its story about the large, terrifying golden statue and chapter 7 with its vision of the Most Holy. Here it can be generally assumed that in the concept of the statue the statement of chapter 7 is already prefigured. The repeated and emphatic use of the figure "four" also indicates an ideal interpretation of history, which is soon pushed into the sphere of metahistory, with the few elements taken from actual history and therefore interpreted from God's point of view as the course of world history prefigured by salvation history, valid beyond time.

A sobering thought is the recognition that, according to the depreciating scale of the metals mentioned in the statue and the description of the four beasts, the course of history, too, is on the decline and that violence and oppression are steadily increasing. Against this dark background is painted the kingdom of God in the guise of the stone which splintered off the rock and became a mountain as well as the vision of the son of man. With him who looks "like a son of man" the "holy ones of the Most High" will reign in the kingdom of God which will come down to earth. We are supposed to recognize in these "holy ones of the Most High" not so much the figures of angels as those of men who are possessors of the new Kingdom of God, who no longer are counted among the chosen people because of blood ties or nationality but because of the high standards of holiness they hold in the name of the new people of God. (Holiness, according to Isaiah, is the essence of God himself.)

The present composition of the book which in some of its statements goes back to the historical figure of Daniel has been in development a long time. It can hardly be assumed that it took its basic form much before 300 B.C., while editorial changes and additions can still be traced to a later period. The author's references to an individual afterlife which assume individual immortality are also worth mentioning (12, 2f) for this last and highest stage of Old Testament revelation.

7. THE MINOR PROPHETS

These comprise a series of twelve unrelated prophetic writings which display individual literary taste. Aside from texts in which the divine spirit can immediately be felt, there are didactic prophetic speeches and even one life story, that of Jonah. They are not called "minor" because their importance and significance are beneath that of the great ones but because the books labeled with their names are much shorter; the term actually goes back to St. Augustine.[4] Their appearance forms the end of the prophets in general: Amos about 760 B.C. in the northern kingdom and the last, Malachi, about 460 B.C., that is, in post-exilic times. Like the great prophets, they share the trait of taking a stand in the face of present-day historical questions, issue commands for the future from their own positions, and thus reveal the future salvific action of God and his kingdom in diverse ways and directions.

8. HOSEA

With few exceptions, the fourteen chapters of this book can be traced back to the most important prophet of the northern kingdom who comes into view about 745 B.C. They are clearly divided into two disparate parts. The first, a symbolic one (1–3), sees the covenant of God with Israel in the marriage of the prophet. The second part (4–14) contains threats and promises for Israel. The book terminates with a hint of future graces and blessings in the coming time of salvation in spite of the lamentations about Israel's infidelity. No other prophet teaches us as much about the fertility rites of Canaan, the first inhabitants of Palestine, as does Hosea. During his time, especially in the northern kingdom, the danger of religious syncretism must have been very great since the worship of Yahweh was imbued with the influence of the Baal rites among all types of people. This also explains the great zeal of the prophet Elijah on behalf of Yahweh. It is from this point of view that we must understand and interpret Hosea.

This holds especially true for the understanding of the first symbolic part (1–3). Traditional interpretation has read these three chapters simply as an allegorical representation of God's love for his people and not as an account based on any personal experiences in the prophet's life. Today, however, exegetes are more and more convinced that according to style and vocabulary the prophet has given an actual account of his married life. The disgrace of marrying a harlot[5] at the demand of God is de-emphasized by a new approach which suggests the feasibility of the fact that every maiden of that time was necessarily subjected to the initiation rites in the temple of Baal in order to secure fertility. In addition such a marriage symbolizes the general state of perversion common to those days. A condition of such long duration needed to be counteracted by emphatic, threatening discourses prophesying disaster and judgment. Only with extreme difficulty can the people fail to react to the prophet's persistence. The symbolic preaching condemns the behavior of the people as a total negation of the covenant conditions: by force of circumstances Israel is dismissed from its privileged state and reduced to the existence of other nations. Yet chapter 2 speaks of a new turn in the future and of a new beginning of the original pure and faithful love of the people for God in a renewed covenant of peace.

Among the threatening utterances in the second part, chapter 2 stands out as a kind of "Canticle of Love" of the Old Testament. It tells that God makes an about-turn in his love of Israel and permits his own justice to be overcome, caused by his sanctity. Hence in this view the prevailing, overall opinion that the God of the Old Testament is the God of Justice and the God of the New Testament is the God of Mercy needs to be corrected.

9. JOEL

We know little more than the name of this prophet and that of his father. The narrative of the four chapters (only three in the Vulgate) is dominated by the description of great, general misery. Chapters 1 and 2 describe a terrible invasion of locusts and a drought with its consequences for men and beasts—reasons enough to appeal for atonement, fasting, and prayers—which of course end with the comforting promise of God's blessings. The second part (3–4) trace in apocalyptic imagery the judgment of the enemies of Israel as a bloody battle, framed by the promise of the outpouring of the spirit upon all people of Israel at the end of time along with a vision of the blessings of paradise for Judah.

These two distinct parts have in the past led exegetes to suspect two different authors. However, a close study of theme, style, language, and last but not least the formal parallel construction indicate rather that we have to do with a unified work which is centered around the idea of the Day of the Lord: 1:15; 2:1f; 3; 4:4; 14. This "day" in the first part carries the features of a limited and passing event, in the second part that of a cosmic and eschatological day of judgment. With like events in both parts, God's inexorable judgment of the enemies is carried out on a historical as well as eschatological plane. The concept of the Day of the Lord which the prophet realizes in the judgment during the scourge of the locusts is transposed and seen in connection with the Last Judgment. Considered this way, the first part outlines the second, eschatological part—which means that the book has to be attributed as a literary unit to one single author, one who can clothe his prophecies in the language of the cult.

There are differences of opinion about the origin of this book. Though it was formerly believed to have originated in the ninth or eighth century before Christ, today's exegetes find that it dates to the time of exile or, considering 4:2–6, even post-exilic times.

10. AMOS

Like Hosea, Amos belongs with the earlier scriptural prophets and is a contemporary of Isaiah. The nine chapters of his book can be thus divided: 1) announcing God's judgment of the neighboring nations, but also of Judah and Israel; 2) warning Israel as to the woes of the coming judgment with a greater persistence in accusations and threats (3–6); 3) describing the five visions about God's patience and the coming judgment (7:1–9, 7); 4) prophesying the reconstruction of the kingdom of David and the coming salvation

(9:8–15). In conclusion it may be said that this small book is so well ordered that, with the exception of a few small additions, it appears to be the authentic work of this prophet.

Amos came from the southern kingdom but finds himself in the northern one. In this we can recognize that God did not condone the separation of the two kingdoms but continues to make his revelation accessible to all of the twelve tribes.

Nowhere as well as in Amos can we discern the immediacy of the prophetic expressions 7:10–17. Yahweh calls him from the status of shepherd to that of a prophet in the northern kingdom. The charisma of the prophetic call is remarkably clear in this text.

11. OBADIAH

This is the shortest of the twelve prophetic books, amounting to only one chapter of twenty-one verses, which first of all contains God's judgment of the Edomites for their crimes in besieging and sacking Jerusalem. This particular judgment in history was to become model and type for the final judgment over all pagan nations. After it the kingdom of God will arise in its infinite greatness. It may be assumed that the book originated in either the exilic or post-exilic times even though the judgment of Edom goes back to the eighth century.

12. JONAH

Whereas the other books of the prophets tell about their visions and report their oracles, the Book of Jonah clothes its prophecies in an episode from the life of Jonah, whose name we encountered in 2 Kings 14:25. The four chapters thoroughly describe Jonah's call from God to preach repentance to Ninive, his attempts to escape the command of God, and his eventual just punishment for this. He is cast overboard and swallowed by a sea monster. Moved by his supplication, God rescues him and returns him to Ninive to preach repentance. This time Jonah obeys, and his preaching in the capital of Assyria brings the desired success. But Jonah becomes bitter over it and God remonstrates with him.

Though the book has a historical figure for its point of departure, it should be considered a didactic story. If we intended to understand the book as real history, it would go far beyond the framework of biblical writings on account of its tremendous miracles. Furthermore, Jonah belongs to the times of the most important king of Samaria, Jeroboam II, according to 3 Kings 14:25 (783–743 B.C.), and it is astonishing to see the lack of any information in the annals of Assyria about Jonah's admonitions to repent for the conversion of Ninive. However, the book teaches God's universal plan of salvation which includes even the worst enemies of Israel, the Assyrians, and fights against a narrow-minded and vindictive mentality of certain Israelites who are intolerant and nationalistic about being the chosen people—whose spokesman Jonah seems to be. God's salvation and mercy are open to all men insofar as they repent and seek forgiveness. During post-exilic times a one-sided religious particularism had made its appearance, and it was in favor of this reform that Jonah's didactic writings were directed with a view to further the teachings of God's salvific plan through the development and continuation of revelation.

Nor is the fact that the contemporaries of Jesus understood this little book so literally and so freely represented its views a proof for the historicity of the report. By using the relevancy of contemporary opinion, Jesus uses this narrative in order to align himself with Old Testament prophecy and to continue building his own revelation upon this basis.

13. MICAH

These seven chapters can be divided into three main parts. The first announces the impending judgment of the Lord with threats against Samaria and Judah, especially against the well-to-do and the evil leaders; only the faithful remnant will be saved. The second part is a promise of consolation centered upon the future salvation which the new David (5:1–3) will prepare as a reign of peace for his people (4, 5). The third part leads from perdition to rescue (6, 7). Most noteworthy here is the trial of unfaithful Israel by God and the pleadings (6:1–8).

The basic form of this book goes back to a younger contemporary of Isaiah around 700, though its present structure was probably acquired in post-exilic times. Micah, who came from peasant stock, lashes out especially against the religious and social evils of Jerusalem. He has in common with Isaiah the messianic hope and the expectation of the

impending reign of peace. Micah 5:1–3 seems
to parallel Isaiah 9:1–5. The well styled
pericope in Micah 4:14 which is also found
in Isaiah 2:2–4 may have been borrowed by
either prophet. But they are a sure indication
that Isaiah as well as Micah expressed the
same hope for the future with the same deposit of ideas.

14. NAHUM

Representing vehement threats of judgment against Ninive, the capital of Assyria,
these three chapters tell in detail how God
appears in judgment and describe the siege
and destruction of Ninive as God's punishment for the many sins of the worldly city.
A dirge for the fallen city terminates the
prophecy.

The book may be dated shortly before the
fall of Ninive in 612 B.C. The prophet,
rightfully indignant over the perversion of
law and the ethical world order by Assyrian
power politics, forecasts the end necessitated
by this.

15. HABAKKUK

The author of this small book of three
chapters cannot be traced to the figure of the

same name in Daniel; rather this prophet is a contemporary of Jeremiah about the end of the seventh century B.C.

The book unites two disparate parts. The prophet bemoans the evildoings of the oppressors and warns of the impending judgment; he describes the advancing enemy. Nor can he understand why the enemy is so utterly cruel; the answer to this is contained in chapter 2. Then follow five lamentations against the bold conqueror. The second part contains a song about the vision of God and describes its effect on the prophet. Of special importance is the pericope (2:1–4) which makes no allusion at all to the time of the Parousia but which makes use of the interim by urging the people to regulate their lives in view of the fact that the Parousia will certainly come. The just man will indeed triumph if he is faithful to God.

16. ZEPHANIAH

We can see that this small book follows the pattern of the prophetic writings: the threat of judgment, the call to repentance, the announcement of salvation. Here the theme covers a devastating judgment of all nations, but especially of Judah. The cultic practices are denounced; those who have gone astray are admonished to repent and return to the fold. Then the consequences of this judgment on Jerusalem and its final rescue are described. The oracle closes by evoking a hymn of joy and praise.

Essentially this book can be traced to the prophet around 630 B.C. This was a time of religious syncretism which brought disastrous effects in its wake during the time of King Manasseh (693–639) and explains the harshness of the prophet's language when he lashes out against the conditions of the times.

17. HAGGAI

An authentic book consisting of two chapters, Haggai has definite origins in 520 B.C. In his four oracles he treats the construction of the post-exilic temple which is the prophet's chief preoccupation. He admonishes and exhorts the people to complete the task; he prophesies the future glory of the new temple and predicts the destruction of the pagan kingdom. Zorobabel, the leader of those who returned from Babylonian exile and the builder of the new temple, is set apart like a signet ring.

18. ZECHARIAH

The works of Zechariah, a contemporary of Haggai, represent the largest of the books of the minor prophets and contain fourteen chapters. It has been established that the first part of the book (1–8) can be traced to the prophet and contains the oracle for the years 520–518. After a brief admonition to repent, there are eight symbolic visions on record which inform the prophet about God's future plan of salvation for all nations. Their apocalyptic character bears references to the Book of Daniel. These visions are explained to the prophet by the so-called interpreting angel; this figure, too, continues to appear in Daniel (1–6). Chapters 7 and 8, in a much different manner, treat a question of fasting and mourning, as well as God's answer to it which is followed by a portrayal of future joys.

Discussion is still rife as to whether or not chapters 9–14 originate with the prophet himself. Some exegetes set an even earlier time while others pick the beginning of the Hellenistic period, that is, the fourth century. Chapters 9–11, with no more worldly kingdoms, tell how the king of peace will appear and how Yahweh will defend his own people.

Chapters 12–14, in texts which at times are indeed impenetrable, describe the future Judah and Jerusalem. We hear of the invasion of the pagans, the diffusion of the spirit, the restoration of the people, the purification judgment on the Day of the Lord, and of the final consecration of Jerusalem.

Compared to the classical pre-exilic prophets, Zechariah's appears as a mere epigone—though such an opinion may be unduly harsh. For even if in many respects he seems to have borrowed his themes from the prophets of the exile, he transforms them and attunes them to his times, a process most vital to the constant development of revelation. Here the concept of messianism in particular is injected with new life (9:9f). He proves that the longing for a messianic king does not disappear with the destruction of the worldly kingdom or with exile, but outlives the shocks of Israel's history in a new way. He also shows that the expectancy of an ideal king cannot be realized within the framework of political history, but is deeply anchored in the religious sphere.

19. MALACHI

The youngest of the twelve prophets wrote

his book of four chapters in 460 B.C., which work can be termed essentially his own. It speaks of God's love of Israel in contrast to his attitude toward Edom. The prophet denounces the priests for their manner of worship and their unjust practices, and promises a new victim. Similar to Esdras, he protests against foreign wives and pleads for fidelity in marriage. He proclaims the Last Judgment for good and evil and adds a final admonition together with the promise that God will send the prophet Elijah in the future time of salvation.

GUIDELINES FOR OLD
TESTAMENT EXEGESIS

I

THE METHODS USED
BY EXEGETES[1]

The exegesis of Holy Scripture is a very di-
versified undertaking to which there are
various working approaches. But only the
original text can serve as a foundation for it,
and even this creates problems since the original texts of the biblical books no longer exist
but are available only in different manuscripts and groupings, or sets, of scrolls (that
is, hand-copied replicas of the original texts).
The critics of the texts strive to reconstruct
the original text from the different, contro-
versial, and incomplete manuscripts. For this
a set of rules has been worked out. Today for
the scientific editions of the Bible we have
developed a method of criticism which co-

ordinates the various deviations from the main text. The exegete from time to time has to decide which of these sources is authentic. In order to do this, of course, he has to have a good knowledge of the general context in order to consult lexicons and concordances and get the meaning of key words and concepts which fit that context. Only by this means will he reach the necessary high degree of competence in the choices he makes so that he will not be too subjective.

Then he has to determine to which literary form his text belongs, and for this he must be familiar with literary criticism. The best known is the literary criticism of the Pentateuch, which has resulted in the present four-form theory (J,E,D,P) and has established its final editions at the time from the tenth to the fifth century B.C. This acceptance as to how the Pentateuch originated came only at the turn of the century, thanks to new discoveries and methods. Form criticism[2] tries to clarify the evolution from the original nucleus of the text to its present form, that is, by projecting backwards in order to sort out the different texts. In connection with the editing history the question is posed as to what caused the various authors who succeeded one another to bring about the present context and what theological points of view are implied therein. Finally, the process of traditional history further points out the literary path taken by the text from its oldest form to the present form and the leitmotif that can be discerned in this development. Needless to say, in spite of the great developmental strides this past forty years, only the bare beginnings have been made, and greater tasks are awaiting the exegete.

If scriptural exegesis heeds these individual aspects, the exegete may interpret his text in the philological-literary manner and find out what the literal meaning of the text may be. But this does not complete his task. According to article 12 of the Constitution "Dei Verbum" of the Second Vatican Council, the biblical scholar must interpret the individual text within the context of greater text units, according to the *analogia* of Holy Scriptures and the *analogia fidei*. This means that he has to put the individual text within the context of the whole Scriptures; he must see the Old Testament in conjunction with Jesus and understand it from his view. He must establish the respective value of the single

117

statement within the collective structure of faith and must interpret it from within it. This further process of research should be regarded as biblio-theological interpretation, which the exegete should not leave to the systematic or practical theologian (fundamental theologian, dogmatician, moral theologian, homeletic theologian, or catechist) as it used to be in the past.

The next question, then, is the meaning of the Scriptures. Today the opinion maintains that the exegete first has to investigate and secure the literal meaning of the text because it contains the intention of the statement by the biblical author which the exegete has to research with the tools of modern exegesis. This literal meaning has the power of proof in theology. Less in German, but much more so in the Anglo-American and Romance language sphere, the exegete also turns, beyond this, to the so-called "sensus plenior," the full sense[3] of Scripture. This means the sense which the individual author did not yet comprehend but which God intended in the announcement of the text. To recognize this, the analogy of Holy Scriptures has to be observed in the interpretation, that is, to accept the position of the individual text in relation to the whole Bible and to understand it. Today we are convinced that a long series of authors as well as communities in the command of God had a part in the origin of Holy Scripture. Thus the task would be to determine the exact value of the individual texts in the different states of development of revelation. According to this, one might equate the task of interpreting Scripture by its "sensus plenior" with a well-understood biblio-theological exegesis. In this connection we must also mention the typological meaning of Scripture,[4] the importance of which again in our times, and especially in Germany, has been reaffirmed by the exegetes. This means that certain factual and verbal statements in the Scriptures are to be referred to later biblical books. Such an interpretation presupposes that the entire Old Testament and New Testament canons are to be taken as a unit and as the essence of revelation history which has happened over the course of two thousand years. This results in the fact that earlier texts remain open toward the future and receive their fulfilling counterparts in later events. Since the revelation development occurs in an ascending continuum, we find the threefold relation of correspondence,

119

surpassing and differentiating between type and antitype. The ways and means, too, of typological Bible interpretation should be called biblio-theological exegesis. At the same time that we endeavor to understand the full meaning of the Scriptures we can recognize in the typological exegesis the path itself which moves from the purely philological to the theological understanding of the Bible.

II

AUXILIARY BIBLE SCIENCES

The complicated exegetical method shown here would never have been possible without a series of auxiliary sciences which were formed in the last century.

We first want to recall Semitic philology. In the nineteenth century the literature of Mesopotamia and Egypt was placed at our disposal. Furthermore, in modern times we found access to several Semitic and non-Semitic dialects spoken in the environment of Israel. We want to make special mention of Ugarit, which was situated to the north of Palestine and left a remarkable literature from the fourteenth to the twelfth century B.C. This fixed a culture which in time and space was closest to the Bible. The comparison of the different languages illuminates various word meanings of established sayings and permits us to understand similes and turns of phrases. Several grammatical constructions and forms achieve better understanding of words and facts.

Archeology takes the lion's share in the discovery of cultures that perished with their literary heritage. It started in the nineteenth century with its excavations in the Near East and in the meantime has obtained the rank of a practical-experimental science. Today the respective cultural institutes of many nations conduct systematic research in Palestine; the Anglo-American countries especially have been pacemakers and continue to be in the forefront of the excavators. As the most important of all we want to mention here the discovery of the Dead Sea Scrolls, which are connected with the name of the French archeologist R. De Vaux. The remarkable fact is the new light they have been shedding upon the early history of Israel and the times of the patriarchs. This has served as a corrective for an all too critical literary criticism which wanted to recognize as genuine only those historical statements for the time after the possession of land in Palestine by Israel, testified to by the Bible.

Hand in hand with the progress of archeology, and as a new source for it, the history of the old East, also that of Israel, has been enriched for several periods of time. Many gaps on the literary map could be filled with content, thanks to different discoveries, most of all that of literary material. Biblical geography, too, is being enlarged and enriched step by step through archeological research. Old highways and streets are being discovered, which helps to a further understanding of some biblical texts.

III

OLD TESTAMENT THEOLOGY

In treating present-day methods of the exegete, we have indicated in many points that it is desirable for the efforts of the exegete to work toward a final understanding of Scriptures from the biblio-theological point of view.

In order to analyze the essence and the tasks of Old Testament theology, it is first necessary to learn something about the history of this relatively young discipline of theology, for its unique course of development mirrors the essence and the tasks of Old Testament theology. During the Middle Ages, and even far beyond them, the whole of Bible science was considered a part of dogmatics. In addition the Bible had the task of preparing the "dicta probantia" for it. Biblical theology, a term which we first find with Ch. Zeller in 1652, attained the character of a separate discipline only in the eighteenth century when interest in the destroyed cultures was reawakened in the age of Romanticism. In his inaugural speech in 1787 in Altdorf, J. Ph. Gabler[1] for the first time suggested and demanded that it be considered a historical discipline. During the following century biblical theology as a historical science entered the main stream of Hegelian philosophy prevailing at that time: that of Hegel's idealism, of natural science evolutionism, determined in the main by Wellhausen, of comparative religion in the age of historical criticism—all these atitudes comprising a criticism without a religious preconception which impressed their stamp on biblical theology up to the twentieth century. These theories are today for the most part outdated and discarded.

Based on Gabler's principles, G. L. Bauer was the first to differentiate biblical theology of the Old Testament from that of the New Testament. With his *Theology of the Old Testament*[2] he opened the way for an independent scientific treatment of Old Testament theology. We shall mention only a few important authors. Among the few adversaries of the historico-critical and grammatico-historical researchers such as W. M. L. deWitte and W. Vatke, we count first J. Ch. K. von Hofmann.[3] At the end of this first important series of developments we find such men as E. Kautzsch[4] and B. Stade. A. Bertholet[5] stands within the circle of historico-evolutionist thinking which contains an empirico-phenomenological representation of Israel's history of religion.

The revolution in theological science after World War I has gradually led to a revival of biblical theology. The relativistic religio-historical consideration has given way to a view which believes in revealed religion and to a theological treatment of the biblical statements. From this newly won point of view, the *Theologies of the Old Testament* by E. König[6] and E. Sellin[7] were written. The true starting point for a factual consideration of Old Testament theology was the appearance of W. Eichrodt's exciting and pace-setting article, "Does Old Testament Theology Still Have Significance Within Old Testament Science?"[8] With this book which soon followed, *Theology of the Old Testament,*[9] he did away with the still valid evolutionary and historical concepts of the past century and prepared the way for a flowering of this noblest discipine of the Old Testament.

The theology of the Old Testament has for its task to research the single books of the Old Testament for their theological content and value. This means to find out, through historical methods, the theologically relevant statements in the different stages of revelation history and to elevate them into the height of revelation obtained at the time as into an immanent bible system. In addition to this it must give a survey of the Old Testament as a whole, to insert the different "fragmentary theologies" such as the ones of the times of the patriarchs or of Moses, into a survey of the Old Testament world of faith. Beyond that, it must order it within the cosmos of theological science as such, present Old Testament theology as part of biblical theology, and point out the function which it has to assume for systematic theology. With this it obtains the position of a link between historical and dogmatic theology that can always fall back upon it as the "never exhausted and therefore always new beginning," as the *norma non normanda.*[10]

This clarifies the fact that Old Testament theology represents the crowning glory of Old Testament science in general; it is the true reason for Old Testament research; all other biblical disciplines do nothing else but prepare the ground for this task: to interpret God's salvific deed and his self-communication within a system that is in accord with the Bible and determined by the Bible content.

In order to do justice to this task, Old Testament theology has constantly to keep in mind the common Semitic and especially the Canaanite background of the religion of Israel, as requested expressly by the encyclical *Divino afflante Spiritu.*[11] In addition it must constantly look back at the New Testament in which the movement of the Old Testament and its most precious powers finally are crystallized. This movement enmeshes the Old and New Testaments into a dynamic, not a static, unity which is fashioned by the arrival and the penetration of the kingdom of God.

In order to fulfill this task it is served, it is true, by the historico-critical method; yet the task cannot be solved purely in a historico-genetic way, but is available only to the comprehension of revealed faith which alone can uncover the foundations and anchor of God's salvific deed. In this, Old Testament theology differs from the religious history of Israel which is mostly concerned with the foundations and developments, as well as the dependence of this religion from the religious concepts of its environment, and therefore hardly recognizes the claim of the Old Testament to contain all revelation reducible to God. Without being personally involved, the religious scientist accepts on a purely statistical basis the material bases of Israel's religion and compares them with others. But in the treatment of the historical and literary problems which appear, he often shows himself tied to assumptions and hypotheses much more than his attested attitude of not being prejudiced will bear out.

The question of the relationship of the Old Testament to the New does not play an important part in the religio-historical considerations.[12] Researchers such as Baumgärtl[13] and Bultmann[14] are convinced that the roots of the New Testament lie in the Old, but they stress the contrast, or rather mutual exclusiveness, between the Old and the New Testaments. In questioning the relationship between the Old and the New, we cannot pay attention merely to the purely historical sequence or to a natural, rationally recognizable development. The relationship must be founded in the supernatural salvation plan of God which theology has to work out and interpret, comprising both the Old and the New Testaments with its center in Christ. In this respect the Old Testament shows an inner tension which is nourished not by natural dynamic forces but by God-inspired entelechies and which presses forward to the fullness of time and the eschaton. This dynamic tension originates in God who carries Old Testament movement of revelation from higher stage to higher stage, realizing his promise from step to step, pursuing his goal which is the establishment of the kingdom of God and with it salvation for mankind. This supernatural dynamic which, like an entelechy, is infused into the history of Israel by God and transforms its profane history into salvation history which is hidden with it and in it at present. Thus the flow of life between the Old and New Testament corresponds to the law of promise and fulfillment, as it can be discerned in the different stages of revelation of the Old and the New in the prominent institution of the covenant of God with man. This movement is aimed at the appearance of the Messiah Jesus Christ in the fullness of time and at the end of time and helps God's kingdom to realize itself deeper and deeper with every stage, until the reign of God at the end of time breaks through in all its glory. In this way the whole Old Testament stands in a messianic-christological frame of reference.

While the religio-historical consideration represents the Israelite religion in its periods according to purely natural developments, the theologically oriented authors in the past have constructed the Old Testament world of faith rather according to systematic categories so as to thus accent the leading ideas and the salvific actions of God. Until the present day the Old Testament theology competes in the different contemporary representations of factual synthesis with the historically conducted analysis trying to find a stabilization. Attempts which take their system of presentation from systematic theology leave us dissatisfied because they do not pay sufficient attention to their own structure and the characteristics of their statements.

Two ways of representation should be specially mentioned here: Eichrodt thus divides the mass of material which he extracts methodically as a cut through the Old Testament world of faith—"God and people, God and world, God and man." He fortunately chooses as his central concept the idea of the covenant. Thus he succeeds in systematizing the theologically important statements gleaned from the structure of the Old Testament into something very close to the Bible itself.

Van Rad[15] has other ideas about the task of Old Testament theology. It is not its task to present the objective course of history in Israel; this still continues to elude our knowledge. Old Testament theology, rather, has the task of retracing the image of salvation history sketched and interpreted in faith by Israel. According to its own law Israel interpreted historical reality each time from the point of faith. Therefore, only this interpretation of history and the subsequent testament of faith for the historical are the objects of Old Testament theology. Admittedly Israel dips much deeper into the background of the historical than will historiography which is critical of the sources. Hence every attempt at systematizing the religious view of the Old Testament is to be rejected. The narrative is the legitimate form of theological language in the Old Testament.

The task of future research might probably consist in starting a fruitful dialogue between the foundations of the typical research methods, as represented by Eichrodt and van Rad, and to develop it into a synthesis of Old Testament theology. Both attempts should be valued as very positive for they are a clear expression of the newly awakened Bible spring of the present.

What, then, of Old Testament theology? It is the transition of the world of faith of the Old Testament into a system which presents the Bible itself and which so places its accents that the graduated importance of the teachings is underlined as the Bible itself requests it. The theology of the Old Testament must work for the inner-biblical growth of the confession of faith, must compare the belief in Yahweh constantly with the religions of Israel's environment, and must lay bare the constantly renewed characteristic of the dynamic flow toward life for fulfillment in the New Testament. Thus it is the crowning termination of Old Testament science, for it prevents exegesis from losing itself in details and making itself absolute; it brings its events into the great overall view and permits it to express itself there.

NOTES

I THE OLD TESTAMENT AS PART OF THE BIBLE

1. See H. Gross, "Zur Offenbarungsentwicklung im Alten Testament," *Gott in Welt:* Festgabe für Karl Rahner (Freiburg-Basel-Wien, 1964) I, 407–422.

I HISTORICAL BOOKS

1. See H. W. Wolff, "Das Kerygma des Jahwisten," *Gesammelte Studien zum Alten Testament* (München, 1964), 345–373; *ibid.,* "Das Kerygma des deuteronomistischen Geschichtswerkes."

2. See H. Rencken, *Uregeschichte und Heilsgeschichte, Israels Schau in die Vergangenheit nach Gen. 1–3,* 2nd ed. (Mainz, 1962).

3. See R. de Vaux, *Die hebräischen Patriarchen Erzählung und die modernen Entdeckungen* (Düsseldorf, 1959); *ibid., Die Patriarchenerzählung und die Geschichte* (Stuttgart, 1965); J. Bright, *Geschichte Israel's* (Düsseldorf, 1966).

4. See also G. E. Mendenhall, *Recht und Bund in Israel und dem Alten Vorderen Orient* (Zürich, 1950) [in English, G. E. Mendenhall, *Law and Covenant in Israel and the Ancient Near East* (Pittsburgh, 1955)]; D. J. McCarthy, *Treaty and Covenant* (Rome, 1963); *ibid., Der*

Gottesbund im Alten Testament (Stuttgart, 1966); K. Baltzer, *Das Bundesformular,* 2nd rev. ed. (Neukirchen, 1964).

5. See H. Graf Reventlow, *Gebot und Predigt im Dekalog* (Gütersloh, 1962); J. J. Stamm, *Der Dekalog im Lichte der neueren Forschung,* 2nd ed. (Bern-Stuttgart, 1962) [in English, J. J. Stamm, *The Ten Commandments in Recent Research* (Naperville, Ill., 1967)]; E. Nielsen, *Die Zehn Gebote* (Kopenhagen, 1965); J. Schreiner, *Die Zehn Gebote im Leben des Gottesvolkes* (München, 1966).

6. See also A. Alt, "Die Ursprünge des israelitischen Rechts," *Kleine Schrift I* (München, 1953), 278–332; E. Gerstenberger, *Wesen und Herkunft des apodiktischen Rechts* (Neukirchen, 1965).

7. See G. von Rad, *Das fünfte Buch Moses* (Göttingen, 1964).

8. *Ueberlieferungsgeschichtliche Studien,* 2nd ed. (Darmstadt, 1957).

9. G. von Rad, *Der Heilige Krieg im alten Israel,* 2nd ed. (Göttingen, 1958).

10. See M. Buber, *"Königtum Gottes," Gesammelte Werke II* (München-Heidelberg, 1964), 485–723.

11. See A. Weiser, *Samuel* (Göttingen, 1962).

12. See O. Plöger, *Theokratie und Eskatologie* (Neukirchen, 1959).

138

I TOBIT, JUDITH, AND ESTHER

1. See H. Gross and H. Schlier, *Die Engel in der Heiligen Schrift* (Leipzig, 1961).
2. See E. Haag, *Studien zum Buche Judith* (Trier, 1963).
3. See D. Arenhovel, *Die Theologie von I and II Makk* (Mainz, 1967).

III THE DIDATIC WRITINGS

1. See A. Arens, *Die Psalmen im Gottesdienst des Alten Bundes* (Trier, 1961).
2. See H. Gunkel and J. Begrich, *Einleitung in die Psalmen* (Göttingen, 1933); P. Drijvers, *Ueber die Psalmen* (Freiburg-Basel-Vienna) [in English, P. Drijvers, *The Psalms, Their Structure and Meaning* (New York, 1965)].
3. See Arens, *Die Psalmen.*
4. S. Mowinckel, *Psalmenstudien I-IV* (Kristiana, 1921–1926), reprint (Amsterdam, 1961) [in English, S. Mowinckel, *Psalms in Israel's Worship,* 2 vols. (London, 1963)]; A. Weiser, *Die Psalmen* (Göttingen, 1959) [in English, A. Weiser, *Psalms* (Philadelphia, 1962)].
5. See W. Richter, *Recht und Ethos* (München, 1966).
6. See L. Krinetzki, *Das Hohe Lied* (Düsseldorf, 1964).

IV PROPHETS

1. See M. Buber, *Sehertum. Anfang und Ausgang* (Köln-Olten, 1950); *Der Glaube des Propheten* (Zürich, 1950).
2. See O. Cullmann, *Heil als Geschichte* (Tübingen, 1965) [in English, O. Cullmann, *Salvation in History* (New York, 1967)].
3. See also H. Gross, "Knecht Gottes im Alten Testament," in F. List, *Seine Rede Geschah zu Mir* (München, 1965) 409–433.
4. See St. Augustine, *De civitate Dei,* XVIII–29; CSEL 40/2, 306.
5. See H. W. Wolff, *Hosea, Biblischer Kommentar,* 2nd ed. (Neukirchen, 1965). Contrary to this we have A. Weiser's opinion, *Das Buch der zwölf Kleinen Propheten I,* 4th ed. (Göttingen, 1963), who interprets Hosea 1–3 as a survey of his failure in marriage; see also W. Rudolf, *Hosea,* (Gütersloh), who interprets the two chapters are referring to two different wives of the prophet.

I. THE METHODS USED BY EXEGETES

1. See *Was heisst Auslegung der Heiligen Schrift?* Contributions by W. Joest, E. Mussner, L. Scheffcyk, A. Vögtle, U. Wilckens (Regensburg 1966); also F. Hesse, *Das Alte Testament als Buch der Kirche* (Gütersloh, 1966).

2. See K. Koch, *Was ist Formgeschichte?* (Neukirchen, 1964).

3. See also R. E. Brown, *The Sensus Plenior* (Baltimore, 1955); P. Grelot, *Sens chrétien de l'Ancien Testament* (Tournai, 1962).

4. See L. Goppelt, *Typos* (Darmstadt, 1966); also G. von Rad, *Theologie des Alten Testaments II,* (München, 1960) 329–424 [in English, G. von Rad, *Old Testament Theology,* 2 vols. (London, 1962–1965)], and H. Gross, "Motiv-Transposition als Form und Traditionsprinzip im Alten Testament," in H. Vorgrimler, *Exegese und Dogmatik* (Mainz, 1926) 134–152 [in English, H. Gross, "Transposition of Themes as Principle of Form and Tradition in the Old Testament," in H. Vorgrimler, *Dogmatic vs Biblical Theology* (London, 1964)].

III OLD TESTAMENT THEOLOGY

1. Published under the title "De iusto descrimine theologiae biblicae et dogmaticae, regendisque recte utriusque finibus," *Opuscula academica II* (Ulm, 1831), 179–198.

2. (Leipzig, 1796).

3. In his main work *Weissagung und Erfüllung* (Nördlingen, 1841) and in *Der Schriftbeweis* (Nördlingen, 1852–1856).

4. *Theologie des Alten Testaments* (Tübingen, 1911).

5. *Theologie des Alten Testaments I-II* (Tübingen, 1905–1911).
6. Fourth edition (Stuttgart, 1923).
7. (Leipzig, 1933).
8. *ZAW* 47 (1929) 83–91.
9. *Zur Zeit* I, II (Stuttgart-Göttingen, 1963/1964).
10. K. Rahner, *Lexikon der Theologie* II, 450 f.
11. *Ueber die zeitgemässe Förderung der biblischen Studien.* Encyclical of Pius XII, "Divino afflante Spiritu," September 30, 1943.
12. See also J. Wellhausen, *Israelitische und jüdische Geschichte,* 8th ed. (Berlin, 1958) [see in English, J. Wellhausen, *Prolegomena to the History of Ancient Israel* (New York, 1957)].
13. F. Baumgärtel, *Verheissung* (Gütersloh, 1952).
14. R. Bultmann, "Weissagung und Erfüllung," *ZTHK* 47 (1950) 360–383.
15. *Theologie des Alten Testaments* I, II (München, 1962/1960) [in English, G. von Rad, *Old Testament Theology,* 2 vols. (London, 1962–1965)].